Here's a book
that lives up to its title

WHITWORTH'S
SPICE
OF
LIFE
COOKERY
BOOK

FOURTH EDITION

Published by Whitworth's Holdings Ltd., Victoria Mills, Wellingborough, Northamptonshire
and Printed in England by Waterlow & Sons Limited, Dunstable and London.

GOOD THINGS TO COOK WITH–

GOOD THINGS TO EAT

Make the most of your recipes by always using WHITWORTH'S FLOUR. Self-Raising or Plain, its perfect quality never varies.

For the same reason you should use WHITWORTH'S whenever a recipe calls for Dried Fruit. Sultanas, Currants, Seedless Raisins. Dried Fruit Mixture. They are all spin-washed and packed and automatically weighed to save you time and work. Whitworth's also pack high quality, ready to use Stoned Raisins and Prunes. Ready Cooked Prunes.

Then there are all the other foods you always like to keep at hand. If they are Whitworth's you can be sure they are the very best:

NUT PRODUCTS
Whole Sweet Jordan Almonds–Whole Blanched Almonds–Roasted Almonds–Ground Almonds–Almond Marzipan–Desiccated Coconut–Nuts and Raisins–Peanut Kernels–Walnut Halves–Brazil Nuts.

GLACE CHERRIES AND CUT MIXED PEEL
Glace Cherries–Mixed Peel.

SUGAR
Sifted Demerara, Soft Brown (Light Golden or Dark).

PRE-PACKED CEREALS, ETC.
Pearl Barley–Butter Beans–Lentils–Macaroni–Medium Oatmeal–Ten-Minit Peas–Dried Peas–Yellow Split Peas–Whole Rice–Long Grain Patna Type Rice–Easy Cook Long Grain Rice–Ground Rice–Flaked Rice–Sago–Semolina–Soup Mixture–Tapioca (Seed, Medium and Flake).

CREAMED RICE MILK PUDDING
The delicious ready-in-a-moment sweet so popular with children.

STUFFINGS
Parsley and Thyme or Sage and Onion, Whitworth's Stuffings are the perfect complement to every kind of poultry.

VARIETY! It's the secret of success in so many things, the spice that adds interest to everyday cooking, just as it does to everyday life.

Not Mrs. Beeton herself, of course, could give every variation of every dish. That's why we've worked out the idea of BASIC RECIPES—recipes to guide you as to the method and principal ingredients for a host of good things.

Learn how to mix and bake a basic Victoria Sponge and you've the trick of a dozen and one delicious cakes. Learn how to handle pastry and what goes into a suet pudding and you can produce endless variations on these tasty themes. You can ring change after change, to suit the season, the ingredients you wish to use and the likes and dislikes of your own family.

Besides our basic recipes, there are many others, plain and party recipes, recipes old and new, together with a collection of hints and short cuts which we hope will save you much time and trouble.

One word more—follow the recipes, especially the basic recipes, as regards method and main ingredients; but don't hesitate to experiment with new seasonings, new flavourings, new variations of your own. All the recipes have been tried and tasted and all have been made with Whitworth's Self-Raising or Plain Flour. This is an ingredient which should not be varied if the best results are to be obtained.

Mrs. Jean Adams,
Cookery Advice Service,
Victoria Mills,
Wellingborough.

*For advice on all questions
to do with cooking, canning, baking and
menu-planning, write to Jean Adams. She will be delighted to
help you in any kitchen difficulties, and to supply information
and special recipes outside the scope of this book. Address
your letter to:—Mrs. Jean Adams, Cookery Advice Service,
Victoria Mills, Wellingborough, NN8 2DT.*

THINGS TO REMEMBER IN USING THIS COOKERY BOOK

All spoonfuls are level ones unless otherwise stated.

Always use large eggs unless otherwise stated.

Here's our Bill of Fare

PASTRY

DELICIOUS RECIPES WITH PASTRY

CAKE MAKING

HOME MADE BISCUITS

ICINGS AND ETCETERAS

SCONES AND QUICKBREADS

BATTERS

PUDDINGS

IDEAS FROM FAR AWAY PLACES

CHILDREN'S SECTION

WEIGHTS AND MEASURES

ELECTRICITY AND GAS
COMPARATIVE TEMPERATURES

For Alphabetical Index of Recipes

turn to the end of the book

INTRODUCTION TO

PASTRY

Why does one woman turn out light, delicious pastry time after time, while another, using the same ingredients and, apparently, the same method and the same oven temperature, regularly produces either hard, dry and uninteresting results or pastry with a soggy underside?

The woman with a light pastry "touch" is lucky but, with knowledge and practice, others can be equally successful. Once the reason for a pastry defect is known, the fault can be remedied. Too much water, for instance, makes a hard crust—too little makes a dry one. Another thing: the more fat there is in the mixture, the less water or other liquid is required.

A general rule in pastry-making (with the exception of hot water paste) is that the ingredients should be as cold as possible and all as nearly as possible of the same temperature.

Here are some other notes which will be useful:

SHORT PASTRY

Fats should be firm—and should be cut into small pieces with a knife before being rubbed into the flour.

Finger tips rather than the palms of the hands should be used in blending flour and fat, because they are cooler. A wire chopper, specially made for the purpose, is better still. This consists of strands of wire attached to a handle to form what is called a "Pastry Blender" which makes a much quicker job of bringing a mixture to the desired fine breadcrumb stage.

Lift the mixture occasionally so that the air gets well into it.

LIQUID is an essential part of short pastry. As has been said, too little—and the pastry is dry. Too much—and it is hard. And remember: the more fat in the mixture, the less water is required.

When you add water to the mixture, do not pour it in in a "lump". as it were, but dot it over the surface.

When adding liquid to the rubbed flour and fat, use the most flexible knife you have and "cut" rather than stir.

Use only enough liquid to make a dough which will roll out easily. Feel the mixture with the finger tips and judge whether or not it requires a little more liquid.

SUET PASTRY

Suet Pastry must be a little moister than short crust pastry.

ALLOW PASTRY TO REST

Too much handling makes close tough pastry, so be as quick and light-handed as possible. And allow all pastry to rest a little before being used, because the necessary movement in mixing it introduces elasticity. If left to rest for a little, there is much less likelihood of the pastry shrinking from the side of the dish or tin and becoming distorted in shape.

ROLLING PASTRY

Don't over-flour your pastry board; excess of flour makes the pastry dry and streaky.

Some cooks roll out pastry between two sheets of greaseproof paper, so that no flour whatever is required. In this way, there is no possibility of lowering the proportion of the fat in the final result by the excessive use of "dusting" flour.

Make the forward rolling stroke the one which really does the work—let the return stroke ride lightly back. This is one of the secrets of light pastry.

GLOSSY PASTRY

When you brush egg or milk over your pastry for glossiness, never wet the cut edges. This would tend to hold it together—you want it to rise or become flaky.

BAKING PASTRY

Bake pastry in a fairly hot oven. Flan shells need about 15 minutes at a temperature of 400-425 degrees Fahr. or gas mark 5-6. Fruit or meat pies should have the heat reduced after a few minutes to allow the fillings to cook.

FLAN SHELLS

Directions for making these are given under Rich Short Crust (page 8). Such shells are baked "blind", as the professional baker says—that is, without any filling.

When lining tins or plates with pastry for flans, see that the rolled-out dough fits closely. The tiniest air pocket left under the crust will expand and spoil the shape of your flan.

FLAN RINGS

For open flans, a flan ring makes for a much more professional job. Place the ring on a baking sheet. Fit the rich short pastry inside it and press it well on to the bottom. Avoid stretching the pastry. Also press the pastry well into the fluted rim, if a fluted ring is used, or well against the sides of a plain ring. Pass the rolling-pin over the top of the ring to cut off excess pastry. Fit greased greaseproof paper, greased side down, into the pastry and fill it with crusts of bread or dried beans or rice. These will help to keep the base flat and also support the sides of the flan.

They and the paper are removed when the pastry is set and the flan is then returned to the oven to finish off the baking. The crusts can be rolled out for topping gratin dishes, while the beans or rice can be used over and over again.

FRUIT AND MEAT PIES

Always cut a vent hole on the top of fruit or meat pies, so that the steam will escape. This keeps the underside of the pastry from becoming soggy.

In a fruit pie, never sprinkle sugar where it will touch the crust, as this, too, leads to sogginess.

To ensure a nice shape for a deep pie, build the fruit up in the centre—remember that it will shrink in cooking. And have the first heat high enough to set the pastry.

FLAKY PASTRIES

Full directions for the making of various flaky pastries are given on pages 7 and 8, but it may be well to review the outstanding points.

Let all the ingredients be of the same temperature. The butter and dough in flaky pastries should be of the same pliability so that they roll out easily. If the butter is too hard, it will be forced through the dough and the flakiness will be lost. If it is too soft, it will not keep in layers, which are what you are attempting to achieve when you roll and fold the pastry from five to seven times.

When rolling out the pastry, try to keep the sides and ends as straight as possible and the corners squared.

Before folding flaky pastry, after rolling it out, give it the very faintest dusting of flour and, if necessary, brush off any excess.

And always rest the pastry after two foldings, if possible. Again, if possible, let the pastry rest for several hours before baking. Pastry which stretches and loses its shape has not rested long enough before being baked.

BASIC RECIPES FOR PASTRY

There are several ways of making flaky pastry and rough puff pastry, but the best of the pastries is that made with an equal weight of fat and flour. The following recipes for two members of the flaky pastry family will give good results.

It is important to give the pastry a half turn after each rolling, because this will keep the layers in line with each other. Never roll over the edges as that would force out the air trapped between the layers and the flaking might be lost.

★ PASTRY, FLAKY (PUFF)

8 oz. Whitworth's Plain Flour
Pinch of salt
8 oz. butter
A few drops lemon juice
Up to ¼ pint cold water

Best results obtainable with Whitworth's Plain Flour but Self-raising Flour can be used without any alteration to recipe.

Sift the flour and salt together. Rub a walnut or so of the butter into them to the fine breadcrumb stage. Add the lemon juice and water and knead until the dough is pliable and well worked together. Knead the remaining butter in the corner of a floured linen cloth to extract moisture and also make the butter the same pliability as the dough.

Roll out the dough to an oblong piece and dot two-thirds of it with half the butter. Bring the unbuttered piece over half the buttered part then bring the remaining buttered part over it. Gently press edges together and then across in parallel lines. This traps and holds the air. Give the pastry a half turn and roll out again to an oblong piece. Use the remaining butter in the same way. This pastry has to be rolled out seven times in all and, if possible, it should be well covered with greaseproof paper and left to rest for 10-15 minutes after each two rollings.

When the pastry is finished, wrap it well in greaseproof paper and again set it aside for at least an hour before using it. Longer would be better. *Note.*—When rolling flaky pastry, try to keep the ends and sides straight and the corners squared.

FLAKY PASTRY TRIMMINGS

For using up the left-over trimmings of flaky pastry, see Jam Turnovers (page 17), Vanilla Slices (page 17) and Palmiers (page 18).
★ *Basic Recipe*

★ PASTRY, ROUGH PUFF

Best results obtainable with Whitworth's Plain Flour but Self-raising Flour can be used without any alteration to recipe.

8 oz. Whitworth's Plain Flour
Pinch of salt
5-6 oz. margarine, butter or lard; or a mixture of any two
A few drops lemon juice
¼ pint cold water

Sift the flour and salt into a bowl. Add the fat (cut in walnut-sized pieces), lemon juice and water. Knead lightly, roll into a strip, and fold in three. Press the edges together, press three times in a row, give the pastry a half turn, then roll out and fold again. Repeat this rolling, turning and folding 5 times, leaving the pastry to stand between the 2nd and 3rd, and 4th and 5th foldings. Roll out and use as required.

★ PASTRY, SHORT CRUST

8 oz. Whitworth's Self-raising Flour
Pinch of salt
4 oz. lard, margarine or dripping
Water to mix

Sift the flour and salt. Rub in the fat, which can be a mixture of lard and margarine, lard and butter or simply plain clarified dripping. When the flour and fat together look like fine breadcrumbs, mix in enough water with a flexible knife to make a stiff but not too dry dough. Use as required—without too much handling.

★ PASTRY, RICH SHORT (OR FLAN PASTRY)

4 oz. Whitworth's Self-raising Flour
Pinch of salt
2 oz. (generous) butter or margarine
1 teaspoon sugar
1 egg yolk

Sift the flour and salt. Rub in the fat. Add the sugar. Mix in the yolk of egg or as much of it as will make a soft pliable dough, reserving enough to brush over the flan. Roll out and line a flan ring or pie tin with the pastry. Be sure to press it well into the bottom of the tin, so as not to trap any air. Make a fancy edge. Prick the bottom with a fork and fit in a lining of greaseproof paper filled with crusts of bread. Bake for 15 minutes in a moderately hot oven (gas mark 5-6 or 400-425 degrees Fahr.). Remove crusts and paper, brush over with egg and return to the oven for a few minutes more.

★ *Basic Recipe*

★ PASTRY, SUET

Suet pastry is to boiled puddings, both savoury and sweet, what short pastry is to everyday meat and fruit pies. It can also be used for dumplings for savoury and sweet dishes.

> *6 oz. Whitworth's Self-raising Flour*
> *Pinch of salt*
> *2½-3 oz. finely chopped suet*
> *Cold water*

Sift the flour and salt together. Mix in the chopped suet (or bought suet already shredded). Add enough water to make a dough which can be handled easily.

★ HOT-WATER PASTRY

Use this pastry for Pork, Veal and Ham, Rabbit (boned) and Game Pies.

> *4 oz. lard*
> *¼ pint water*
> *12 oz. Whitworth's Plain Flour*
> *½ teaspoon salt*

Best results obtainable with Whitworth's Plain Flour but Self-raising Flour can be used without any alteration to recipe.

Boil the fat and water together to melt the fat. Sift the flour and salt into a warmed bowl to take off the chill. Stir in the liquid. Work with a wooden spoon until cool enough to handle, then knead well. Cover and keep in a warm place so that it will remain pliable.

★ CHOUX PASTRY

This is used for Cream Buns (page 16), Eclairs (page 16), Profiteroles (page 16) and Gateau St. Honoré (page 51).

> *½ pint water*
> *2 oz. butter or margarine*
> *5 oz. Whitworth's Plain Flour*
> *Pinch of salt*
> *3 eggs*

Bring the water and butter to the boil. Add the sifted flour and salt all at once, then stir and beat briskly until the mixture is smooth. When it leaves the side of the pan, remove, cool slightly, then beat in the eggs, one at a time.

★ *Basic Recipe*

9

DELICIOUS RECIPES WITH PASTRY

LEMON MERINGUE PIE

> 1 baked flan shell, 6-7 in. across
> 4½ oz. sugar
> 1½ oz. Whitworth's Plain Flour*
> A few grains salt
> ½ pint boiling water
> ½ oz. margarine or butter
> 2 eggs
> Juice and grated rind of 1 large or 1½ small lemons
> 3 oz. caster sugar

Have ready the flan or pie shell made of short crust (page 8). Mix the sugar, flour and salt in a bowl. Add the boiling water. Stand in a pan of boiling water and cook for 15 minutes. Add the fat. Blend the egg yolks, lemon juice and rind and stir them gradually into the hot (but not boiling) mixture. Turn into the baked shell.

Whip the egg whites very stiffly. Lightly fold in the caster sugar and spoon the mixture on to the filled pie. Bake in a moderately slow oven (gas mark 2-3 or 325-350 degrees Fahr.) for 20 minutes or until the meringue is a delicate biscuit colour.

Note.—For a crisper meringue, sprinkle with a little caster sugar and bake up to 30 minutes.

*Cornflour may be used instead, but use a little less.

EGG WHITES AND YOLKS

Where a recipe calls for egg yolks only, the whites can be used in Meringues or Meringue toppings for fresh Fruit Tarts, Apple Meringue and Queen of Puddings, or for Baked Alaska, Angel Cake, Snowdrop Cake, Cats' Tongues, Jap Cakes and Macaroons. (For page numbers, see Index.)

Egg yolks left over when the whites only are used in a recipe can be used in Flan or Rich Short Crust Pastry, in Buttercup Cake, Vanilla Pastry Cream or to replace water in Digestive Biscuits. (See Index.) Also used for such sauces as Mayonnaise, Bearnaise or Mousseline.

ORANGE MERINGUE PIE

Follow the previous recipe but use the grated rind and juice of 1 orange and 1 teaspoon lemon juice in place of the lemon. Reduce the sugar to ½ teacup.

★ CUSTARD PIE

> *Short Crust Pastry (page 8)*
> *2-3 eggs*
> *½ pint hot milk*
> *1 tablespoon sugar*
> *A few grains of salt*
> *A few drops vanilla essence*
> *A sprinkling of grated nutmeg*

Make the short crust pastry with up to 3½ oz. fat to 6 oz. Whitworth's Self-raising Flour. Roll out the pastry very thinly and cut off a circular band for the rim of the pie plate or tin. Wet the rim and place the strip of pastry on it. Wet the top of the strip and line the plate with the remaining pastry, pressing it well and closely on to the bottom and sides. Prick the bottom with a fork. Lightly press together the two layers of pastry on the rim. Decorate the edges with a fork or the finger and thumb and leave to rest for half an hour.

For the custard filling: Beat the eggs just enough to combine them well. Stir in the hot milk, then add the sugar, salt and vanilla essence. Brush the inside of the pastry with a little egg white saved from the eggs in the custard (about a teaspoonful is ample). Strain the custard into the pastry, sprinkle with grated nutmeg, then bake for 10-15 minutes in a hot oven (gas mark 6 or 425 degrees Fahr.). Reduce the heat to gas mark 4 or 375 degrees Fahr. for the remaining time (30 minutes in all).

Variation I: **Demerara Custard**
When taken from the oven, at once sprinkle the custard pie with a good teaspoonful of Whitworth's Demerara crystals.

Variation II: **Almond Custard Pie**
Use 2 eggs only and mix into the strained custard a good tablespoonful of Whitworth's ground almonds.

Variation III: **Coconut Custard Pie**
Add 2-3 tablespoons Whitworth's desiccated coconut to the strained custard.

Variation IV: **Pumpkin Custard Pie**
Use ¼ pint milk only and add to the custard 1 teacup sieved steamed pumpkin and a tiny pinch each of ground ginger, cinnamon and cloves.

★ *Basic Recipe*

11

TWO-CRUST APPLE PIE

Two-crust plate pies are more often made with apples than with other fruits, but apples with dates or sultanas, blackberries and apples, gooseberries, rhubarb—indeed all the fruits you would use in deep pies—are perfectly good in shallow ones. The difference is that, in shallow two-crust pies, no water is added to the fruit.

For shallow two-crust pies, use short pastry (page 8). Roll out the bottom piece as thinly as possible and place it in the pie plate. Add half the fruit, then sugar to taste, then the remaining fruit. Cover with the pastry rolled out to less than ¼-inch thick, first wetting the rim of the bottom piece. Trim the edges, gently press them together and mark with a fork or a knife. Cut one or two short slits on top. Bake for 35-45 minutes (according to size) in a moderately hot oven (gas mark 5-6 or 400-425 degrees Fahr.).

MINCEMEAT TART

The two-crust pie recipe, above, can be used with a mincemeat filling. Use 12 oz. to 1 lb. mincemeat in a deep plate or sandwich tin about 9 in. diameter. Make a stock of mincemeat according to the following recipe:—

MINCEMEAT

8 oz. Whitworth's currants
8 oz. Whitworth's sultanas
8 oz. Whitworth's stoned raisins

       OR
Two 12 oz. packets of
Whitworth's Dried Fruit Mixture

1 lb. peeled grated cooking apples
12 oz. Whitworth's soft brown sugar
6 oz. shredded suet
4 oz. Whitworth's cut mixed peel
½ level teaspoon ground cinnamon
½ level teaspoon ground nutmeg
¼ pint. brandy or rum optional

Mix all the ingredients together in a large basin. Cover and leave overnight. Pack into sterilized jars. Cover tightly and keep for about one month before using.

DEEP FRUIT TARTS

Make short pastry and roll it out ¼ inch thick. Place the inverted pie-dish on top and cut out a piece of pastry slightly larger than the outline of the dish. Next, cut out a long strip of pastry the length and width of the dish's rim. Wet the rim and place the strip on it, without stretching. *(Stretched pastry shrinks during baking.)*

Half fill the pie-dish with the fruit. Add sugar according to the tartness of the fruit. If it is very dry, add a tablespoonful or two of water. Add more fruit, building the centre well up to allow for settling while cooking; or put in a pie support. Now wet the top of the pastry rim and lay the ready-cut piece on top of it. Note that the slightly larger size of the piece cut out for the top now fits because of the heaped-up fruit. Trim off surplus pastry, slanting outwards. Cut laterally into the edges of the pastry and draw in shallow scallops with the tip of a sharp knife. Cut a small slit in the centre with a sharp knife, brush with syrup, if you like, and bake for 30-40 minutes in a moderately hot oven (gas mark 5-6 or 400-425 degrees Fahr.).

Note.—For the syrup, dissolve 1 teaspoon sugar in 2 of water.

STRAWBERRY PIE

Apple, blackberry and apple, gooseberry, plum, raspberry and rhubarb deep pies or tarts are all favourites, but deep strawberry pie—almost the most delicious of all—is seldom made. Do decide to make at least one of these during the season. A mixture of small fruits such as gooseberries, raspberries and red currants is also very good, and so are apricot or peach pies. Any bottled fruit can be used when fresh fruit is not available.

TREACLE TART

Line a greased large pie tin or plate with short pastry. Prepare the filling by mixing 3 tablespoons golden syrup with 2 oz. breadcrumbs or crushed Weetabix. Add ½ teaspoon ground ginger. Spread this in the lined tin and bake for 20 minutes in a moderately hot oven (gas mark 5-6 or 400-425 degrees Fahr.).

ECCLES CAKES

> *8 oz. Flaky or rough puff pastry (page 8)*
>
> Filling:
>
> *4-5 heaped tablespoons Whitworth's currants*
> *1 oz. Whitworth's chopped candied peel*
> *¼ teaspoon grated orange or lemon rind*
> *1 tablespoon Whitworth's Demerara sugar*
> *1 teaspoon lemon juice*
> *¼ teaspoon mixed spice (if liked)*
> *1 oz. melted butter*

Have the ingredients for the filling warmed ready in a bowl. Roll out the pastry to ¼ inch thick and cut into rounds about 4 inch in diameter. Divide the filling between the rounds, placing it on the centre of each. Damp the edges and gather them together in the centre. Pass a rolling-pin very lightly over each. Place, joined side down, on a greased tin. Brush with a little egg or milk and sugar and prick with a fork. Bake for 18-20 minutes in a hot oven (gas mark 6-7 or 425-450 degrees Fahr.).

Note.—Alternative quick fillings for Eccles Cakes are 4-6 tablespoons of Dried Fruit Mixture moistened with lemon curd.

MINCE PIES

1 lb. mincemeat (page 12)
12-14 oz. short, flaky or rough puff pastry

Roll out the pastry and stamp it into small rounds with a cutter.

Place half the rounds on a greased baking tin and put a good tea-spoonful of mincemeat on each. Wet a border all round with water or beaten egg, place a matching piece of pastry on top and gently press into position.

Decorate the edges with a fork, supporting them with the flat of a knife. Brush with beaten egg and pierce with a fork.

Or place the bottom rounds in lightly greased patty tins and follow the above directions.

Bake short pastry for 20 minutes in a hot oven (gas mark 6-7 or 425-450 degrees Fahr.), and flaky and rough puff pastry for 20 minutes in a very hot oven (gas mark 8 or 475 degrees Fahr.).

Sprinkle the mince pies with sugar when they come from the oven.

BAKEWELL TART

Short crust pastry (page 8)
Raspberry, blackcurrant jam or
Lemon curd
2 oz. butter or margarine
2 oz. caster sugar
1 large or 2 small eggs
2-3 oz. Whitworth's ground almonds or cake crumbs
1-2 drops almond essence
A little milk, if necessary

Roll out the pastry very thin. Cut a strip the length and width of the rim of the pie tin or plate. Wet the rim of the tin and place the strip on it. Then line the tin with the pastry, taking care not to have a bubble of air in the centre, and first damping the pastry rim.

14

Cream the butter and sugar very well. Beat in the egg (or eggs) until the mixture is very light, then fold in the ground almonds or cake crumbs with almond essence. Add about a tablespoon of milk, if the mixture needs it.

Spread a layer of jam or lemon curd on the bottom of the pastry-lined tin, and put the batter on top. Bake for 25-35 minutes in a moderately hot oven (gas mark 4-5 or 375-400 degrees Fahr.), or until the "cake" is a golden brown.

WELSH CHEESE CAKES

6 oz. rich short crust pastry or rough puff pastry (page 8)
Jelly or jam
4 dessertspoons caster sugar
4 tablespoons Whitworth's ground rice or Whitworth's
*   fine semolina*
2 tablespoons melted butter
1 good-sized egg

Roll out the pastry and line 9-12 small patty tins with it. Into each, place a tiny teaspoon of jelly or jam. Mix together the sugar, ground rice or fine semolina and melted butter. Lastly, stir in the well-beaten egg. Place on the jam in small spoonfuls and bake for 15-20 minutes in a fairly hot oven (gas mark 6 or 425 degrees Fahr.).

JAM TART

Short crust pastry (page 8)
Jam

Roll out the pastry quite thin and line a pie tin or plate with it, pricking the bottom well. Spread with jam, as thickly as you wish. Roll out the trimmings and cut into ½-inch strips. Twist them and lay them across the jam, damping the edges and fixing them to the pastry underneath. Now cut a strip the length and width of the tin's rim. Damp the rim and place the strip over it and the joined edges of the twisted strips.

Pinch together in a fancy pattern or fork the edges—or twist the strip of pastry and lay it on the damped surface of the rim. Bake for 25 minutes in a hot oven (gas mark 6-7 or 425-450 degrees Fahr.).

CREAM BUNS

Place good teaspoons of Choux Paste well apart on a greased baking-sheet. Cover with a deep roasting tin and bake for 40 minutes starting with a hot oven (gas mark 6-7 or 425-450 degrees Fahr.) and turn down to moderately hot (gas mark 5-6 or 400-425 degrees Fahr.) after 15 minutes.

Place on a wire rack and at once make a slit in the side of each to allow the steam to escape. When cold, pipe sweetened vanilla-flavoured whipped cream or confectioners' custard (page 17) into each bun.

ECLAIRS

Place the Choux Paste in a piping bag fitted with a ½ inch pipe and pipe 3½-in. lengths on to a greased baking sheet. Bake for 35-40 minutes in a moderately hot oven (gas mark 5-6 or 400-425 degrees Fahr.). Split to allow steam to escape and, when cold, fill with cream as above. Ice with chocolate glacé icing, if desired, or dust with icing sugar.

PROFITEROLES

Place hazelnut-sized pieces of the Choux Paste, well apart, and bake for 20-25 minutes in a hot oven (gas mark 6-7 or 425-450 degrees Fahr.). Open at the side and, when cold, fill with sweetened and flavoured whipped cream. Heap in a serving dish and pour chocolate sauce (page 84) over them.

CREAM HORNS

½ lb. rough puff or flaky pastry (pages 8 or 7)
Raspberry or apricot jam
Whipped cream or synthetic cream

Roll out the pastry to ⅛ in. thick and about 9 in. long. Cut into 1-in. strips. Brush with beaten egg yolk and place, brushed side out, on greased cornet tins, the pastry overlapping enough to form a join. Bake for 15 minutes in a hot oven (gas mark 7 or 450 degrees Fahr.).

Remove from the tins. When cold, place a little jam inside and pipe in the cream.

JAM TURNOVERS

Roll out rough puff or flaky pastry trimmings very thin. Cut into 4½-in. squares. Place a teaspoon of jam in the centre of each. Dampen a narrow margin, fold over crosswise and press a little. Brush with beaten egg, avoiding the cut edges. Bake for 18-20 minutes in a hot oven (gas mark 6-7 or 425-450 degrees Fahr.).

MAIDS OF HONOUR

> ½ lb. flaky pastry
> 1 teacup sour milk curd
> 2 oz. melted butter or margarine (cooled)
> 1 egg
> 2 oz. sugar
> Grated rind of small lemon
> 2 oz. Whitworth's ground almonds
> 1 small tablespoon fine breadcrumbs
> Pinch of grated nutmeg
> A few drops brandy or vanilla essence

Roll out the pastry to one-eighth inch thick. Cut into rounds and fit closely into tartlet tins. Beat the filling ingredients together and fill the pastry with them. Bake for 20-25 minutes in a hot oven (gas mark 7 or 450 degrees Fahr.).

VANILLA SLICES

Roll out ½ lb. flaky or rough puff pastry to one-eighth inch thick and cut to fit your baking sheets. (You can use the upturned bottoms of baking tins instead). Bake for 10-15 minutes in a hot oven (gas mark 7 or 450 degrees Fahr.). Remove and cool.
Make **Confectioners' Custard** by melting 1 oz. butter in a saucepan. Blend in 1 oz. plain flour and simmer for a minute. Remove and stir in ¼ pint milk. Return to the stove and cook for 2-3 minutes. Cool a little, then add 1 oz. sugar and beat in 1 egg yolk. Cook gently, without boiling, for another minute, adding a little more milk if the custard seems too thick. Finally, stir in ½ teaspoon vanilla essence.
Spread one layer of pastry with pipless raspberry jam, then spread the cold custard ½ inch thick on top. Cover with the other piece of pastry, bottom up so as to get a level surface, and ice. Leave until firm, then briskly cut into suitable oblongs with a sharp knife.
Variation:
Instead of custard, use thick whipped cream, sweetened and flavoured with vanilla.

PALMIERS

Place trimmings of flaky pastry one on top of the other, to keep the flaking in the correct position, then roll them out very thinly indeed to form an oblong or strip with one side about 18-20 inches long. Trim. Brush lightly with cold water, sprinkle the surface with caster sugar, then fold the two ends over, almost to meet in the centre. Pass the rolling pin lightly over the pastry. Sprinkle with more caster sugar and fold in the same two ends again. Roll lightly. Sprinkle with sugar and fold again down the middle so that the original 18-20 inch side has been reduced to about 2-3 inches.

Leave to rest for a little, then cut into very narrow slices (less than ¼ inch thick) with a very sharp knife. Place well apart on a baking sheet and bake for 10-15 minutes in a hot oven (gas mark 7 or 450 degrees Fahr.).

YOUR OVEN AND YOUR TINS

It will pay you to buy baking tins which utilise your oven economically.

Try this: Take a shelf from your oven and place the tins you already have on it. You may find that you cannot bake two sandwich tins on the one shelf because they are a trifle too large. That may be why you are never quite pleased with your sandwich cakes. The top one may be baked perfectly but, because you have to place the other on the shelf below, it may never be quite so well baked and may not rise so well.

It may be better to buy a pair half inch less in diameter because you can then place the two tins on the one shelf at the same time.

This applies to loaf tins. If you want to make 4 rich fruit cakes at the one time, buy tins which can fit together on the one shelf and your cakes will be much more uniform than if 2 were baked on one shelf and 2 on another.

Then there are pudding dishes. Oblong or oval ones will use oven space far more economically than round ones because they reach further back into the oven, so that you can get 2 of them on one runner instead of one. You can, therefore, use both oven space and fuel to better advantage.

FRUIT FLANS

These are some suggestions for filling the flan cases for which directions are given on pages 5, 6 and 8.

APRICOT FLAN

Poach enough halved fruit to fill the flan in syrup (1 teacup water and 1-2 tablespoons sugar boiled for ½-minute). Place the fruit in the flan. To the syrup (just under ½-pint) add 1 teaspoon arrowroot blended with a little water. Bring this to the boil, let it cool a little and pour it over the apricots. If you like, pipe a little cream around the cold flan.

CHERRY FLAN

Use poached, bottled or tinned cherries for the flan filling. If the cherries are red, add a drop of cochineal to the syrup.

GREENGAGE FLAN

Follow the apricot flan recipe, but leave the greengages whole.

PEACH FLAN

Follow the apricot flan recipe, first skinning the peaches. Use them halved or sliced.

STRAWBERRY FLAN

Choose enough uncooked ripe strawberries to cover the bottom of the flan, halving them if necessary. Pack them fairly closely. Mash ¼ lb. of the ripest strawberries, add a little water and bring to the boil. Rub through a sieve and sweeten to taste. Return to the pan and add a teaspoon arrowroot blended with a little water to a cupful. Bring to the boil, allow to cool slightly, then pour over the strawberries. Decorate with cream piping or serve with whipped cream.

19

SAVOURY PASTRY DISHES

RAISED PIES

Raised pies are many people's first choice for special cold-meal occasions. They are made with what is called "hot-water pastry" (page 9) because the fat is boiled in water to dissolve it, then stirred into the flour and kneaded to a smooth easily-handled paste. After a piece has been reserved for the lid, the paste is raised to form a case for the contents of the pie.

Have the paste still warm enough to mould easily. Place a round of it on a board. Work a depression in the centre with the knuckles of one hand and, at the same time, with the other hand, gradually raise the sides to form the case or shell of the pie. After packing in the meat, wrap 2-3 thicknesses of greaseproof paper round the pie to support it, then put on the lid and bake the pie.

Or the pie can be baked in a cake tin or in one of those hinged tins specially made for these pies.

If you feel that moulding by hand is not an easy way to make the case, you can work the paste over the bottom and sides of a tin slightly smaller than you are going to bake the pie in. Slip off the case and transfer it to the larger tin. How to get the paste off easily? Pour hot water into the tin and at once out again, then lift out the tin and leave the moulded case, ready to be filled.

★ PORK PIE

> Hot-water pastry (page 9)
> 1½ lb. lean pork
> Pepper and salt
> 1-2 hard-boiled eggs
> 2-3 tablespoons water
> A teaspoon or so best quality powdered gelatine
> (Enough for 6 or 7 helpings)

Make the pastry as above. Cut off a quarter for the lid and mould the remainder into the pie case. Chop the meat and season it well, adding, if liked, ½ teaspoon mixed dried herbs. Fill the pie with the meat and the sliced hard-boiled egg or eggs. Add the water. Roll out the piece for the top. Damp the edges of the pie, place the top in position and pinch together. Make a hole in the centre.

Cut "leaves" from the pastry trimmings. Brush the top of the pastry with beaten egg and place the leaves in position. Brush them with egg

★ *Basic Recipe*

and bake for 2-2¼ hours in a moderate oven (gas mark 4 or 375 degrees Fahr.).

Make a savoury stock with pork bones, a little water and an onion. Dissolve the gelatine in a small cup of the strained stock. Pour hot into the hot pie through a funnel in the central hole. Serve cold with salad.

Variation I: **Rabbit and Pork Pie**
Use rabbit meat and pork, half and half, and follow the above recipe.

Variation II: **Veal and Ham Pie**
Use equal amounts of veal and ham and proceed as above. Be careful with the salt as the ham may be salty.

Variation III: **Grouse, Partridge or Pigeon Pie**
Bone the bird and cut the meat into suitable pieces. Add enough full-pork sausage meat to make up the required amount, then proceed as for Pork Pie.

BACON AND EGG ROLL

12 oz. short crust pastry (page 8)
1 breakfastcup sliced barely cooked potatoes
4 rashers of bacon, cut into strips
2-3 sliced skinned tomatoes
1 teaspoon chopped parsley
A few grains Cayenne pepper
Salt to taste
2-3 eggs
¼ pint of milk
(Enough for 4 helpings)

Reserve 2-3 oz. pastry for trimmings. Roll out the remainder to a largish oblong, less than ¼ in. thick. Down the centre, place the potatoes, bacon, tomatoes, parsley and seasoning in layers, leaving a margin all round. Damp this margin, then wrap the pastry round the filling, sealing the edges well. Turn over so that the join is underneath. Make a small hole in the centre and pour the beaten egg and milk through it into the filling, reserving a little.

Roll out the reserved pastry and cut out some "leaves" from it. Brush the whole of the visible roll with some of the egg and milk saved and decorate with the "leaves" while the surface is still wet. Brush more beaten egg over them, then bake for 20-30 minutes in a hot oven (gas mark 6-7 or 425-450 degrees Fahr.).

QUICHE LORRAINE

> *4 oz. short crust pastry (page 8)*
> *1-3 oz. lean bacon (scalded)*
> *2 eggs*
> *2 oz. grated cheese*
> *1 small onion*
> *½ oz. butter or margarine*
> *A few grains Cayenne pepper*
> *1 breakfastcup (scant) milk*
> (Enough for 4 to 6 helpings)

Line a flan or shallow pie tin with the pastry. Cut the bacon into inch-wide strips and slice the onion finely, fry gently in the butter without browning. Turn into the pastry case. Beat the eggs and mix them with the remaining ingredients. Pour over the bacon and bake for 35-40 minutes in a fairly hot oven (gas mark 4-5 or 375-400 degrees Fahr.).

Note.—To scald the bacon, pour boiling water over it, leave for a minute, then drain.

Variation I: **Swiss Flan**
In place of bacon, have a layer of thinly sliced potatoes, then proceed as above.

Variation II: **Onion Flan**
In place of bacon, slice and blanch two good-sized onions. Drain well. Cover the bottom of the flan with them and proceed as above.

CORNISH PASTIES

> *6-8 oz. short crust pastry (page 8)*
> *½ lb. lean steak*
> *1 breakfastcup diced raw potatoes*
> *1 chopped onion*
> *1 tablespoon water*
> *Pepper and salt to taste*
> (Enough for 4 pasties)

Roll out the pastry and cut into 4 saucer-sized rounds. Mix together the finely chopped meat, potatoes, onion, water and seasoning to taste. Place a portion in the centre of each round of pastry and wet the edges. Form into half moons and pinch together in a fluted edge. Brush with milk or beaten egg yolk, prick each side with a fork and bake for 50 minutes in a fairly hot oven (gas mark 4-5 or 375-400 degrees Fahr.).

22

HOLLAND

BUTTER CAKE

½ lb Butter

½ lb Soft Brown Sugar.

1 level teaspoon finely grated lemon peel.

1 Standard Egg.

½ lb Plain flour.

2 ozs Blanched chopped almonds

Method:

1) Cream butter, sugar, lemon peel until light & fluffy.

2) Beat in egg; gently fold in flour

3) Spread into Swiss Roll tin (approx 8" × 12") Scatter almonds over the top

4) Bake in centre of moderate oven, Gas 4 for 45 to 50 mins (or until Golden)

5) Remove from oven

Cool slightly & cut into Squares or
fingers -

6. Store in an airtight tin when cold

MUTTON PIES (SCOTCH)

Make hot-water pastry (page 9).
Put aside one-third of it for the tops of the pies. Mould the remainder into 5-6 shallow raised pies (page 20). Or (much simpler) line 5-6 deep patty tins with it.
For the filling use:

> *¾-1 lb. lean mutton*
> *Pepper and salt*
> *Pinch of mace optional*
> *Stock from the bones*

Remove the bones from the meat, cover them with water, add seasoning to taste and simmer until a nice rich stock is obtained. Cut the meat into small pieces or put it through a coarse mincer. Season with pepper and salt and, if liked, mace. Moisten with the stock. Fill the prepared cases with this mixture. Roll out the remaining pastry and cut into tops to fit the pies. Cut a small hole in the centre of each. Wet the edges of the main pastry, put on the tops and pinch together. Bake for 35-40 minutes in a moderately hot oven (gas mark 5-6 or 400-425 degrees Fahr.). Using a funnel, pour a little of the boiling well-seasoned stock into each pie and serve hot.

Variation:
Good quality sausage meat and a slice of hard-boiled egg per person make tasty individual pies.

BEEFSTEAK AND KIDNEY PIE

> *¾ lb. flaky, rough, puff or short crust pastry (pages*
> *7 and 8)*
> *1¼ lb. stewing steak*
> *2 sheep's kidneys*
> *½ tablespoon flour*
> *½ teaspoon salt*
> *Pinch of pepper*
> *Water*
> (Enough for 4 or 5 helpings)

Cut the meat and kidneys into suitable pieces and coat them with the flour, sifted with the seasoning. Barely cover with water and simmer very gently for 2½ to 3 hours.
Meanwhile, roll out the pastry. Invert the pie-dish on it and cut a piece slightly larger than the top. Then, following the line of the dish, cut a strip wide enough for the rim. Wet the rim of the dish and place the band of pastry on it.

(continued overleaf)

23

Place a pie funnel in the centre of the dish with the meat around it. Add enough cold gravy almost to come through. Damp the top of the pastry rim and place the other pastry on it. With a sharp knife, cut off the edges, holding the knife in an outward slanting position so that the pastry is a little over the edge of the rim. This allows for a little shrinkage. With the back of the knife, knock up the cut edges to encourage rising. Brush with beaten egg, avoiding the cut edges. Make a small hole where the pie funnel touches the pastry.

Roll out the pastry trimmings and cut out "leaves" with a fancy cutter. Place them around the centre hole and the edges of the pie. Brush with beaten egg. Bake flaky or rough puff pastry for 30 minutes in a hot oven (gas mark 7 or 450 degrees Fahr.) and short crust pastry for 35-40 minutes (gas mark 6 or 425 degrees Fahr.). When the pastry is a warm gold, cover the top with greaseproof paper.

Note. – The meat should almost fill the dish.

SAUSAGE ROLLS

> *½ lb. rich short crust or flaky pastry (pages 7 and 8)*
> *½ lb. sausage meat*

Roll out the pastry ⅛ in. thick, in a long narrow strip just wide enough to encircle the sausage meat. Form the meat into a roll as long as the pastry and place it along the centre of the strip. Damp the edges, wrap the pastry round the meat and press edges together. Cut into suitable lengths and place, joined sides down, on a baking sheet. Brush with beaten egg or milk.

If short crust is used, bake for 20-25 minutes in a hot oven (gas mark 6-7 or 425-450 degrees Fahr.). If flaky pastry is used, bake in a hot oven (gas mark 6-7 or 425–450 Fahr.).

Variation:

Instead of sausage meat, use minced or chopped corned beef, seasoned with 1 teaspoon chopped parsley and a pinch each of thyme and marjoram.

★ TWO-CRUST MEAT PIE

> *8 oz. short pastry (page 8)*
> *1½ breakfastcups minced cooked meat*
> *1-2 tablespoons rich gravy*
> *Seasoning to taste*
> (Enough for 4 or 5 helpings)

Roll out half the pastry and line a pie plate or tin with it. Fill with the well-seasoned meat and gravy. Tinned meat or left-over meat from a joint are equally suitable. Roll out the other half of the pastry, cover the pie and trim off. Make a few slits on top. Use the trimmings for decoration. Brush with beaten egg or milk and bake for 30-35 minutes in a hot oven (gas mark 6 or 425 degrees Fahr.).

★ *Basic Recipe*

Variation I: **Corned Beef Hash Pie**
Use 3-4 oz. chopped corned beef and cubed parboiled potatoes for filling. Season well.

Variation II: **Vegetable-Meat Pie**
Grate a teacup carrots and 1 onion and mix these with a small cup of minced cooked meat. Season well and proceed as above.

MERINGUES

In certain cakes, only the yolks of eggs are used and the left-over whites must then be utilised for other purposes. Suggestions for this are given on page 10. Here is another one: Meringues, to be sandwiched with whipped cream, when ready.

For each egg white, allow 2 oz. caster sugar.

As egg whites will not whip if there is the slightest trace of grease on the whisk, the first thing to do is to wash both the whisk and the bowl with a soapless detergent, rinse very well and dry thoroughly.

Whip the egg whites very stiffly so that, when you invert the bowl, they remain where they are and do not slip in the least.

This is most important because, if the whites are not thoroughly whipped, the meringues will spread instead of holding their shape. Sprinkle the top with half the required amount of sugar and whip well again, then lightly fold in the remaining sugar. Have ready a clean very lightly oiled baking sheet. Shape the meringues with two dessertspoons or tablespoons this way:

Dip one spoon in cold water, shake off the water and take up a spoonful of the meringue mixture. With another spoon, dipped in cold water and shaken, spoon out the meringue on to the prepared baking sheet. Sprinkle with caster sugar. Repeat until all is used.

Place the meringues in a very cool oven and leave them there for 4-5 hours when they should be completely dry all through. Have the temperature in an electric oven at 200 deg. Fahr. In a gas oven, use the lowest setting and dry for about 2 hours.

CREAM OF MUSHROOM FLAN

6 oz. short pastry (page 8)
3 oz. mushrooms (pale gills)
1 oz. butter or margarine
A few drops lemon juice
1-2 tablespoons water
1 teacup top milk
1 heaped teaspoon cornflour or rice flour
Salt to taste
A few grains Cayenne pepper
(Enough for 4 helpings)

Line a flan tin with the pastry and bake it for 15 minutes Peel and slice the mushrooms. Melt the fat, add the lemon juice and water and bring to the boil. Add the mushrooms, cover tightly and cook for 5 minutes. Add the milk, reserving a little in which to blend the cornflour. Stir in the blended cornflour or rice flour and simmer for 3-4 minutes. Turn into the baked flan shell. "Leaves" of pastry (from the trimmings) can be baked with the pastry and used for garnishing.

EGG AND CABBAGE PIE

1 tablespoon butter or margarine
1 small chopped onion
1 breakfastcup chopped heart of cabbage
½ breakfastcup Whitworth's cooked rice
2 chopped hard-boiled eggs
Pepper and salt to taste
8 oz. short pastry (page 8)
(Enough for 4 to 6 helpings)

Melt the fat and simmer the chopped onion in it. Pour boiling water over the cabbage, cook gently for 5 minutes, drain and add to the onion. Cook gently together for a further 7-8 minutes, being careful not to brown. Stir in the rice. Remove from heat and add the hard-boiled eggs and seasoning to taste. Allow this mixture to cool. Divide the pastry into 2 pieces. Line a shallow pie plate with one. Put in the cold prepared filling. Roll out the other piece of pastry and cover the pie with it.
Trim and pinch the edge into a fluted rim. Brush with beaten egg yolk or milk, decorate with the trimmings and brush them, too. Bake for 25-30 minutes in a hot oven (gas mark 6-7 or 425-450 degrees Fahr.).

★ BEEFSTEAK AND KIDNEY PUDDING

½-¾ lb. suet crust pastry (page 9)
1 lb. lean stewing steak
2 sheep's kidneys or 4 oz. ox kidney
1 good tablespoon flour
Pinch of pepper
½ teaspoon salt
1 tablespoon chopped parsley (optional)
(Enough for 4 or 5 helpings)

Roll out the pastry and line a greased quart pudding basin with three quarters of it.
Cut the meat and cored kidneys into smallish pieces and roll them in the flour and seasoning. Add the parsley and turn into the lined basin with enough cold water to come just below the level of the meat. Wet the edges of the pastry. Pat out the remaining piece to the size of the top of the basin, place it in position and pinch the edges together. Cover with greased greaseproof paper, twisting this under the rim to make a good closure and tie a cloth on top. Have ready a saucepan with boiling water deep enough to reach halfway up the basin. Put in the pudding, put on the lid and boil *hard* for at least three-quarters of an hour. After this the heat can be lowered, but the water must be kept boiling since suet crust becomes heavy if the water is allowed to go off the boil. Fill up pan with boiling water as necessary. Boil for 3 hours in all. Then remove the cloth and paper, wrap the basin in a napkin and serve. When you cut the pudding, pour in as much extra gravy as it will take, adding more as you serve the pudding.

Variation I: **Beefsteak and Mushroom Pudding**
Replace the kidneys with ¼ lb. halved or quartered mushrooms. Use field mushrooms for finest flavour and do not peel them if they are in good condition. Simply wipe them over with a cloth.

Variation II: **Beefsteak and Tomato Pudding**
Instead of mushrooms in the above recipe, use 2 or 3 tomatoes skinned and chopped.

Variation III: **Beefsteak and Vegetable Pudding**
Use a half pound instead of a pound of meat and add a handful of butter or haricot beans previously put to soak overnight. Parboil these and mix them with the meat together with 1 or 2 diced carrots and sliced onion.

★ *Basic Recipe*

27

CHICKEN PUDDING

Suet Pastry (double the quantities given on page 9)
1 boiling fowl
4 oz. pale-gilled mushrooms
Seasoned flour
Water
(Enough for 5 or 6 helpings)

Line a greased pudding bowl with three-quarters of the pastry. Cut the chicken into suitable pieces, boning the legs and the larger part of the carcass. Put the bones, neck, skinned feet and giblets (except the liver which should be reserved for breakfast) into a stewpot and cover with cold water. Add an onion, a bouquet garni, some parsley roots, pepper and salt and a small glass of cider. Cover and cook slowly for several hours.

Roll the pieces of chicken in flour seasoned with pepper and salt and, if you like, ¼ teaspoon grated nutmeg. Place in the lined bowl. Add the mushrooms, cut in quarters, and a squeeze of lemon juice, then pour in enough of the strained cold chicken stock to come just below the level of the meat. Wet the edges of the pastry. Roll out the remaining piece, place it on top and pinch the edges together. Cover with greased greaseproof paper and tie on a cloth. Stand the bowl in a pan of boiling water reaching half-way up and boil for 3-3½ hours. Have the remaining hot strained stock from the bones ready. When the first piece of crust is cut out, pour in as much stock as the pudding will take; and, as the pudding is served, keep on adding the delicious stock or gravy.

Variation: **With Rabbit**

Rabbit can be used in exactly the same way as chicken for a delicious savoury pudding. Parboil it first for five minutes and then wash it well to get rid of any strong flavour.

STEAMED PUDDINGS

A cloth is not necessary for puddings which require no more than 2-3 hours' steaming. Simply cover them with 2-3 thicknesses of greaseproof paper, twisting them around and under the rim. No string is required.

PUFF-PASTRY CASES
and FILLINGS

Whether you want tiny little bouchees, measuring about a five-shilling piece in diameter (1½in.), for a cocktail party, or small individual vol au vents generally known as "patties", or large vol au vents sufficient for 3-4 persons, all are made in the same way.

Briefly, this is what to do:

Roll out the flaky pastry to the required thickness, as given in the following recipes, then cut or stamp out a round or rounds of the pastry with a plain or fancy cutter. If you use a plain cutter, make quite sure that you do not turn it as that would make the pastry cases rise lopsidedly.

Next, with a smaller cutter to suit the size of the vol au vent or pastry case, cut part way through so that, when the pastry is baked, you can lift off the "lid" and remove any uncooked pastry which may remain inside. This must be done as soon as the cases are taken from the oven because, if you leave them to become cold, you will not be able to remove each lid in one piece. Your case or cases are now ready for the filling. You can make these pastry cases early in the day—or even the day before you require them—then simply heat them through before putting in the hot filling.

VOL AU VENT *(for 4 Servings)*

1 lb. flaky pastry (page 7)
Filling (see below)

Roll out the pastry to between ¾ and 1 inch thick. Then, with an oval or round pan lid held just touching it with one hand, mark the outline of the lid on the pastry. Next, with a very sharp knife, cut through to the board. Place the pastry on a wet baking sheet and, with the same sharp knife, cut three-quarters way through it ¾-1 inch inside the outer edges.

Brush with beaten egg, avoiding the cut edges, and bake for 25-35 minutes in a hot oven (gas mark 7 or 450 degrees Fahr.). In a gas oven, lower the heat 1 mark after 20 minutes and, in an electric oven, lower it 25 degrees after 15 minutes.

Lift off the lid and remove any gelatinous pastry inside. Fill with the hot filling, replace lid and serve.

29

BOUCHEES

Roll the pastry out between ⅓ and ½ in. thick.
These are the very tiny vol au vents measuring 1½-2 inches across.
Stamp out the rounds, then cut halfway through each with a tiny
cutter. Brush with beaten egg, avoiding the cut edges, and bake for
10-12 minutes in a very hot oven as above. Proceed as for the large Vol
au Vent.

PATTIES (INDIVIDUAL VOL AU VENTS)

Individual vol au vents are more tidy to serve, though not so spectacular
at table as one large one.

1 lb. flaky pastry (page 7)
Filling

Roll out the pastry to between a third and under half an inch thick. Cut
out rounds with a plain or fluted 3-3½-inch cutter. Place on the wet
baking sheet and press about three-quarters through each with a
2-2½-inch cutter. Brush with beaten egg, avoiding the cut edges, and
bake as above for 20-25 minutes. Proceed as for the large Vol au Vent.

VOL AU VENT FILLINGS

CREAMED CHICKEN

1 breakfastcup cooked chicken in small pieces
1 cup creamy white sauce (page 124)
Seasoning to taste
1 egg yolk and 1-2 tablespoons cream (optional)

Add the chopped chicken to the sauce, made, if possible, with half
chicken stock and half milk. Season well, using a few grains of Cayenne
pepper, if you wish. If you use the egg yolk and cream, beat them
together just to blend and stir into the other mixture. Heat through but
do not allow to boil. Fill the hot case or cases with the hot mixture,
replace the lid or lids and serve at once.
Note.—A teaspoonful of sherry, added to the white sauce as you make
it, is a great improvement.

CREAMED LOBSTER

Follow the above recipe using flaked cooked lobster instead of chicken.

CREAMED MUSHROOMS

1½ cups medium thick creamy white sauce (page 124)
4 oz. small pale-gilled mushrooms
1 oz. butter
1 teaspoon lemon juice
1 tablespoon water
Seasoning

Make the seasoned white sauce. Wash the mushrooms, but do not peel them. Cut them into thin slices. Place the butter, lemon juice and water in a small lidded pan and bring to the boil. Stir in the mushrooms, cover and cook for 5 minutes. Add to the creamy sauce with, if you like, an egg yolk blended with a tablespoon of cream. Heat through but do not boil. Fill the hot case or cases with the hot mixture, replace lid or lids and serve.

OTHER FILLINGS

Diced left-over meats such as veal or lamb or flaked cooked white fish, especially sole or turbot, are all excellent for Vol au Vent fillings when blended in a creamy sauce as above. For an extra pleasant flavour, add a pinch of curry-powder to the sauce, but not enough to make it noticeable.

HOW TO BLANCH NUTS

To blanch almonds, walnuts or pistachios for puddings and cakes, drop them into boiling water for half a minute or so and the skins will then come off very easily. You can use them, blanched, just as they are, or brown them in the oven in the first place.

For Salted Nuts: *Pour 2 tablespoons of edible oil into a frying-pan. Add 2-3 oz. blanched nuts and heat slowly until they become a pale gold. Drain and place in a paper bag with a tablespoon of fine salt. Shake the nuts in the bag until well coated with the salt. Remove and place in a baking tin lined with greaseproof paper. Dry off in a cool oven.*

NOW WE COME TO
CAKE-MAKING
WITH A SPECIAL WORD ON
CAKE-BAKING

"She makes the most marvellous cakes"—Do people say that about you? They will, when you follow Whitworth's basic cake recipes and ring delicious changes to suit the occasion and the ingredients you wish to use.

If you know how to make a good Victoria Sponge Sandwich, you have the secret of every cake made by the creaming method.

A B C OF CREAMING AND BEATING

(*a*) When a recipe tells you to *cream* the fat, it means just that. Beat the fat until it is soft and creamy.

(*b*) When the sugar is added, beat again—and beat well—until the mixture is light and fluffy.

(*c*) When you are told to beat in one egg at a time or a little beaten egg at a time, the idea is to avoid curdling or separating the mixture. Should the mixture separate, you lose much of your work because the air you have beaten into the fat and sugar simply slides out. So watch closely and, if there is any indication that the mixture may separate, sprinkle in a tablespoon or less of the flour and go on beating.

An alternative method is to beat the eggs and then beat them in, a little at a time. Another way is to sprinkle a tablespoon of the flour over the creamed mixture before adding the eggs. There is still another way in which the egg whites are whipped separately and, last thing, folded in over and over after the flour has been mixed in. This last applies only to cakes without fruit.

Spices should be sifted with the flour so that they will be evenly distributed. Flavourings, too, will be better distributed if they are added after the first lot of flour.

DRIED FRUITS

You can now buy Whitworth's finest washed currants, sultanas and seedless raisins for your cakes and puddings. In addition to these fruits, there are also Whitworth's Stoned Raisins and Whitworth's Dried Fruit Mixture, consisting of currants, sultanas, seedless raisins, lemon and orange peel.

Inside the title page there is a complete list of Whitworth's top quality range of foods packed and weighed automatically without a hand touching them.

WHY FRUIT FALLS

There are several reasons why fruit falls to the bottom of a cake. One is when the mixture is too moist or the fruit itself too damp. Another is when the temperature in the oven is too low. A third reason is when the fruit is added in advance of the flour. It becomes coated with the sugary fat, which, when heated, causes the fruit to slip right through the cake to the bottom.

This last is why it is so difficult to keep glacé cherries in position. If the cherries are very syrupy, they should be wiped in a really damp cloth to remove the sugar which, otherwise, will become a thick syrup in the cake and cause the fruit to sink. The following method has proved successful: Sprinkle 2 oz. flour through the cut-up cherries, leave for 2-3 hours or overnight, then turn into a sieve and shake out excess flour. *(See* Cherry Cake, page 53.)

Add fruit to a cake mixture *after* the final lot of flour has been added.

A final word about fruit cakes: If you have an electric mixer, use it only for creaming the butter and sugar, then simply stir in the beaten eggs alternately with the flour and add the fruit last of all. This is because a fruit cake is not intended to be a light cake and, if it is beaten as you would a Victoria Sponge or fatless sponge mixture, the weight of the fruit will cause it to sink more than is allowed and your cake will have a decided dip in the centre.

THE RUBBING-IN METHOD

This method is generally used for the less rich cakes. Here the fat is rubbed into the sifted flour and salt, as for short crust pastry. The fat may be butter, margarine, lard or dripping. Cut it in pieces into the flour, then rub it in with the tips of the fingers. The fruit, sugar and spice, if used, are then added and, finally the eggs and milk or water are stirred in.

Too much liquid will make a soggy cake and too little a dry rocky one. Rock Cakes (page 60) are an instance where the mixture must be dry, as otherwise they will not hold their shape.

Cut-and-come-again Cake (page 41) is an example of a "rubbed-in" cake.

"PEAKED" CAKES

When your cake peaks or "boils out", it means that your oven was too hot when the cake was put in. This is what happens: the outside crust sets and hardens before the cake has risen because the heat has not had time to get through to the centre. When it does reach the centre, it causes the mixture to expand and, as it must go somewhere, it cracks the top and "boils out" if the top crust is firm; or simply pushes its way up into a peak if the top is not strong enough to withstand it.

WHEN A CAKE IS BAKED

In spite of given temperatures and careful timing, be quite sure that your cake is cooked before you take it from the oven. There are various tests for "readiness".

First, there is the test by ear. When cakes made by the creaming method are done, they are silent. Up until then, a slight hissing sound come from them. Test this way: Carefully draw the cake on its runner from the oven, bend down and listen. If there is no hissing or if the cake does not "sing at you", you can safely remove it. But, if it does "sing", return it to the oven for a few minutes longer.

A second test is to place your third finger gently on the middle of the cake top. If a depression is left on the surface, return the cake to the oven. But go very gently with this kind of test because it could° cause the cake to drop. This test is for both creamed mixtures and fatless sponges.

Another indication that a cake is baked is when there is a slight shrinkage all round.

The old method of testing a cake with a smooth skewer is not necessarily a reliable one, although an experienced cake-maker will know by what clings or does not cling to the skewer whether the cake is baked or not. The danger of this test is that one is very apt to damage a fruit cake because the skewer may "run into" a piece of the fruit and this in itself will often be the cause of a heavy, if not fallen, cake.

OTHER POINTS

Anyone who can mix a good cake should be able to bake it, but this does not always follow. Study the instructions which come with your cooker and make sure you understand your oven temperatures before you begin.

A cake is properly baked only when the whole of the outside is evenly coloured not too dark and not too thick and "crusty".

A dark crust indicates too hot an oven. A thick crust is caused if the cake is left over long even in a coolish oven.

You can also get a dark crust while the centre of the cake is sunk; this indicates too hot an oven and a mixture which is too dry.

A cake will sink if you bang the oven door before the mixture has had time to set. Heavy-footed people stumping around the kitchen will also produce the same effect. An over-wet cake, too, will fall and be soggy in the centre, as the moisture takes too long to evaporate.

A rich cake, which may be perfectly baked, sometimes tends to settle, but do not confuse this with sinking.

A dry cake may be dry because it was left too long in the oven, even at a low temperature; or the fruit used may have been so dried out that it took away moisture from the cake. That is why it is advisable to use Whitworth's washed and cleaned dried fruit, packed in prime condition and ready to use straight from the packet.

GLYCERINE

Glycerine can be a most useful addition to cakes and also to Royal Icing (page 82). Added to cakes, it helps to keep them moist. Allow a teaspoon to each half pound of flour, beating it in after the eggs and before the flour.

For Royal Icing, allow a dessertspoon for each pound of icing sugar. This will prevent the icing from becoming too hard.

"IDENTICAL-TWIN" CAKES

If you want Victoria Sponge Sandwiches and any other layer cakes to have each layer identical, weigh the two tins, one against the other, using both sides of your scales, and make allowances for any difference in weight so that the two tins balance each other exactly. Divide the cake mixture evenly between them and again weigh them to be sure that the one balances the other. Your cakes, when baked, will then be exactly alike.

35

★ VICTORIA SPONGE SANDWICH

4 oz. butter or margarine
4 oz. caster sugar
2 large eggs
4 oz. Whitworth's Self-raising Flour
Pinch of salt

Have ready greased and floured two sandwich tins measuring 6½-7 inches across.

Cream the fat and sugar fairly well, until light, but do not over-beat. Sprinkle a tablespoon of the flour over the surface, then beat in the eggs, one at a time, taking care that the first is well beaten in before adding the next. Sprinkle the sifted flour and salt on top and stir in as lightly as possible, making sure that the mixture is well incorporated.

Divide between the two tins and level off. Bake for 20-25 minutes in a moderate to moderately hot oven (gas mark 4-5 or 375-400 degrees Fahr.). Turn on to a cake rack and leave to cool out of a draught. Sandwich with seedless raspberry jam or apricot puree and sprinkle with icing sugar. Alternately sandwich with one of the fillings on page 85.

Note.—Some folk like to add a tablespoon of warm water to Victoria Sponge. If you follow the above recipe and the eggs are not a good size, add the water after the eggs are well beaten in. Some people also find that, by beating in the beaten eggs a little at a time instead of whole eggs one at a time there is less likelihood of the mixture separating.

"EQUAL WEIGHT" VICTORIA SANDWICH

If preferred, instead of weighing the fat, sugar and flour in 4 oz. each, weigh the eggs and have their weight in each of the other three ingredients. In this way you make sure that you have a properly balanced mixture.

This is, of course, the French "Quatre-Quatre."

Variation: Chocolate Sponge

Use only 3-oz. flour well-sifted with a pinch of salt and 1 oz. cocoa or chocolate powder. Add ½ teaspoon vanilla essence with the eggs. If a really dark cake is desired, add a few drops liquid gravy browing with the eggs. Sandwich with Vanilla Butter Icing (page 86).

Note.—In addition to cocoa a good pinch or two of instant coffee improves the flavour.

★ *Basic Recipe*   36

★ MADERIA CAKE

> 6 oz. Whitworth's Self-raising Flour
> Pinch of salt
> 4 oz. butter or margarine
> 4 oz. caster sugar
> Grated rind of ½ lemon
> 2 good-sized eggs
> Milk to mix

Sift the flour and salt. Cream the fat and sugar, then add the grated lemon rind to them. Beat a heaped tablespoon of the flour into the mixture. Add the eggs, one at a time, beating the first well in before adding the second. Beat in a portion of the remaining flour, then add the rest in several portions. Mix well to give a smooth texture and a firm dropping consistency, adding a little milk, if required.

Turn the mixture into a greased and floured 6 in. to 6½ in. tin and bake for 1 hour to 1 hour 10 minutes in a moderate oven (gas mark 3 or 350 degrees Fahr.), lowering the heat slightly after 50 minutes if necessary.

Note.—If desired, place a very thin slice of citron peel on top of the cake once it has set. If this is done in the first place, the peel may sink.

Variation I : **Fruit-Spice Cake**

Sift ½ teaspoon mixed spice and ¼ teaspoon ground cinnamon with the flour. Lastly, add ½ to ¾ lb. Whitworth's Dried Fruit Mixture. Omit the citron peel. Bake 45 minutes at above temperature then for a further 30-45 minutes at a lower setting (gas mark 2 or 325 degrees Fahr.).

Variation II : **Ginger Cake**

Sift 2 teaspoons ground ginger with the flour. Omit the citron peel. Bake as for Madeira Cake.

Variation III : **Seed Cake**

Add 2 teaspoons caraway seed with the first flour and omit the citron peel.
Bake as for Madeira Cake.

Variation IV : **Sultana Cake**

Add ½ to ¾ lb. Whitworth's sultanas and omit the citron peel.
Bake as for Fruit-Spice Cake.

★ *Basic Recipe*

WALNUT CAKE

> 4 oz. butter or margarine
> 4 oz. caster sugar
> 3 eggs
> 4 oz. Whitworth's Self-raising Flour
> 1 oz. cornflour
> Pinch of salt
> 1½ oz. Whitworth's finely chopped walnuts

Grease and flour a 6½-7-inch tin.

Cream the fat and sugar very well. Beat in 2 whole eggs, one at a time, and the yolk only of the third. (The white is used for the frosting.) Sift together the flours and the salt and mix the walnuts into them. Add to the creamed mixture. Turn into the prepared tin, level off and bake for 55 to 65 minutes in a moderate oven (gas mark 3-4 or 350-375 degrees Fahr.).

Turn on to a cake rack. When cold, coat with American Frosting (page 80). Pour all the frosting at once on top of the cake and, with a palette knife, quickly spread it over and around the sides, finishing off with a swirl over the top. This must be done quickly. Immediately place 7-9 halved walnuts around and in the centre of the top.

Note.—If preferred, bake the cake in two 6½-inch sandwich tins, giving them 20-25 minutes at gas mark 4-5 or 375-400 degrees Fahr. Ice, when cold, using a little of the frosting for the filling.

COOLING CAKES

Rich fruit cakes are better left in the tin until they are almost cold before turning them out. They will then not crumble.

Cakes of the Victoria Sandwich type should, if necessary, be gently loosened all round with the tip of a knife. Place a wire rack over the tin and then invert it. In a second or two, the tin can be lifted off easily. This includes cakes of the Madeira type.

A true sponge cake—that is, a fatless sponge—should be left in the tin until nearly cold, then turned on to a rack to finish cooling.

A sponge sandwich should be turned on to a sugared paper immediately it is baked.

An Angel Cake should be turned on to a wire rack and left in the tin to become cool, when it will drop out on to the rack itself.

★ ALMOND CAKE (ECONOMICAL)

> *2 oz. margarine*
> *2 oz. lard*
> *4 oz. caster sugar*
> *2-3 eggs*
> *2 level tablespoons golden syrup*
> *10 oz. Whitworth's Self-raising Flour*
> *¼ teaspoon salt*
> *½ teaspoon almond essence*
> *¼ teaspoon lemon essence*
> *¼ teaspoon bicarbonate of soda*
> *Up to ¼ pint fresh or sour milk*

Grease and flour a dripping tin, approx. 7 x 11 in.
Cream the fats and sugar very well. Sprinkle 2 tablespoons of the flour on top. Beat in the eggs, one at a time, then the syrup. Beat well. Add half the sifted flour and salt and the essences, then the remaining flour and the soda blended with the milk. (If sour milk is used, beat it and the soda well together before adding.)
Turn into the prepared tin, level off and bake for 1 hour in a moderate oven (gas mark 3-4 or 350-375 degrees Fahr.).
Variation I: For a **Fruit Cake,**
add 1 lb. Whitworth's Dried Fruit Mixture and increase baking time about ¼ hour, at a slightly reduced temperature.
Variation II: For a **Dark Fruit Cake,**
use brown sugar and black treacle instead of caster sugar and golden syrup. Or add a few drops of liquid gravy browning or caramel.

ALMOND CAKE (RICH)

> *6 oz. butter or margarine*
> *6 oz. caster sugar*
> *4 oz. Whitworth's ground almonds*
> *4 eggs*
> *8 oz. Whitworth's Self-raising Flour*
> *Pinch of salt*
> *A few drops almond essence*

Cream the butter and sugar very well. Work in the ground almonds. Beat in the eggs, one at a time (a little of the flour, if necessary), then add the sifted flour and salt and the almond essence. Turn into a greased and floured 7½-8 in. tin and bake for 1 hour at gas mark 3 or 350 degrees Fahr., then reduce the heat to gas mark 2 or 325 degrees Fahr. and bake for a further ½ hour.

★ *Basic Recipe*

GINGER FRUIT CAKE

8 oz. Whitworth's Self-raising Flour
½ teaspoon salt
1 teaspoon ground ginger
½ teaspoon ground cinnamon
3 oz. fat
3 oz. caster sugar
1 egg
1 good tablespoon black treacle
¾ cup sour milk (or ⅜ pint)
¼ teaspoon bicarbonate of soda
1 cup Whitworth's sultanas or raisins

Sift together the flour, salt and spices. Cream the fat and sugar. Add the egg and beat well. Beat in the treacle and about a quarter of the dry ingredients. Stir together the milk and soda. Add some of this to the main mixture, then the sultanas or raisins, then the remaining dry ingredients and, finally, the rest of the milk and soda.

Turn into a greased and floured oblong tin 7½ in. x 11½ in. and bake for 35-40 minutes in the centre of a moderately hot oven (gas mark 4-5 or 375-400 degrees Fahr.).

Note.—For a slightly richer cake add an ounce or two of cargo ginger cut into small pieces, together with an ounce or two of chopped walnuts.

★ ALBERTA DATE CAKE

4 oz. chopped stoned dates
½ pint boiling water
¼ teaspoon bicarbonate of soda
4 oz. butter or margarine
6 oz. caster sugar
½ teaspoon salt
2 eggs
10 oz. Whitworth's Self-raising Flour
¼ lb. Whitworth's chopped walnuts

Chop the dates and soak them for 1 hour in the boiling water. When cool, stir in the soda.

Cream the fat, sugar and salt until light. Beat in the eggs, one at a time. Stir in half the flour, then the almost cold dates and water, then the remaining flour and the walnuts. Turn into a greased and floured tin, 7 in. x 11 in., and bake for 1 hour in a moderate oven (gas mark 3-4 or 350-375 degrees Fahr.).

★ Basic Recipe   40

GINGER DATE CAKE

Add a sifted teaspoon ground ginger and ½ teaspoon mixed spice with the flour. Follow the directions for Alberta Date Cake (page 40).

CUT-AND-COME-AGAIN CAKE

> *8 oz. Whitworth's Self-raising Flour*
> *¼ teaspoon salt*
> *4 oz. dripping or margarine*
> *4 oz. caster sugar*
> *¼-½ teaspoon mixed spice or grated nutmeg*
> *4-6 oz. Whitworth's Dried Fruit Mixture*
> *1 oz. Whitworth's chopped candied peel*
> *2 eggs*
> *1-2 tablespoons milk*

Sift the flour and salt and rub the fat into them until as fine as for short crust pastry. Add the sugar, spice, dried fruit and peel. Beat the eggs and add with the milk.

Have ready greased and floured a deep tin about 6 in. in diameter. Turn the mixture into it and level it off. Bake for 1½ hours in a moderate oven (gas mark 3 or 350 degrees Fahr.). Or, in a shallow tin, bake for 30-40 minutes at a slightly higher temperature.

Note.—For a dark and richer cake, use brown instead of caster sugar.

MYSTERY CAKE

> *4 oz. butter or margarine*
> *10 oz. Whitworth's Self-raising Flour*
> *½ teaspoon mixed spice*
> *¼ teaspoon grated nutmeg*
> *1 teaspoon cinnamon*
> *¼ teaspoon salt*
> *6 oz. Whitworth's soft brown sugar*
> *6 oz. Whitworth's Dried Fruit Mixture*
> *4 oz. Whitworth's walnuts*
> *A generous ¼ pt. milk*

Grease and flour a 7 in. cake tin. (Set oven at gas mark 2 or 300-320 degrees Fahr.).

Chop the walnuts, sieve the flour with the spices and salt, rub in the fat until the mixture resembles breadcrumbs. Stir in the brown sugar, making sure there are no lumps. Stir in the fruit and walnuts and thoroughly mix to a fairly soft consistency with the milk.

Put into the prepared tin and bake for 1¾-2 hours.

HONEY SANDWICH CAKE

4 oz. butter or margarine

2 oz. Whitworth's soft brown sugar

2 level tablespoons thick honey

6 oz. Whitworth's Self-raising Flour

2 eggs

4 tablespoons milk

Grease and flour, or line, a 7 in. cake tin. (Set oven at gas mark 4 or 350-375 degrees Fahr.)

Cream the butter, sugar and honey together until they are soft and light. Gradually beat in the eggs, adding a little sieved flour if the mixture shows signs of curdling. Fold in the sieved flour and milk to give a soft consistency.

Put into the prepared tin and bake for 45 min. When cold this cake can be split and layered with butter icing (page 86) or, for a change, why not try one made with honey?—as follows:—

2 oz. butter

2 oz. sieved icing sugar

1 level tablespoon thick honey

Cream the butter well and beat in the sugar and honey.

SAND CAKE

6 oz. butter

6 oz. caster sugar

3 eggs

½ teaspoon Vanilla essence

4 oz. cornflour

4 oz. Whitworth's Self-raising Flour

2-3 tablespoons milk to mix

Grease and flour a 2 lb. loaf tin. (Set oven at gas mark 3 or 350 degrees Fahr.)

Sift the flour and cornflour together. Cream the butter and sugar together until soft and light. Gradually add the egg and Vanilla essence. Fold in the flour and cornflour. Lastly add the milk to give soft dropping consistency.

Spread into the prepared tin and bake for 1¼ hours or until firm.

RICE CAKE

Use 4 oz. of Whitworth's Ground Rice in place of the cornflour in the above recipe. Proceed as above.

★ SPECIAL CAKE

> *3 oz. butter*
> *4 oz. caster sugar*
> *3 oz. Whitworth's Self-raising Flour*
> *Pinch of salt*
> *2 large eggs*
> *1 tablespoon lukewarm water*
> *Vanilla essence to taste*

Cream the butter and sugar very well, then work the sifted flour and salt into them. Whisk the eggs thoroughly and stir into the mixture. Finally, add the water and vanilla essence. Turn into a well-greased and floured tin, 6-6½ in. across, and bake for 40-50 minutes in the centre of a moderately hot oven (gas mark 4-5 or 375-400 degrees Fahr.).

Variation I: **Chocolate Cake**
Melt 1 oz. sweet chocolate in 1 dessertspoon hot water and blend it into the other ingredients with the vanilla.

Variation II: **Coffee Cake**
In place of the vanilla essence, add ½-1 teaspoon coffee essence. Or add a level teaspoon of dry atomised coffee with the flour.

CHOCOLATE LAYER CAKE

Make the Chocolate Cake mixture as above. Turn into two greased and floured 6-7-inch sandwich tins and level off. Bake for 20-25 minutes in the top of the oven at the same temperature. When cold, sandwich with vanilla or coffee butter icing (page 86).

COFFEE LAYER CAKE

Follow the Chocolate Layer Cake recipe, using the Coffee Cake mixture.

★ *Basic Recipe*

DEVIL'S FOOD CAKE (EGGLESS)

1 rounded tablespoon black treacle
13-14 tablespoons hot water
3 oz. margarine or lard
8 oz. Whitworth's Self-raising Flour
¼ teaspoon salt
3 oz. caster sugar
1 oz. cocoa
¼ teaspoon vanilla essence
¼ teaspoon coffee essence
¼ teaspoon bicarbonate of soda

Grease and flour two 7-in. sandwich tins. Add the treacle to the hot water and leave to dissolve. Melt the fat and leave to cool. Sift the flour, salt, sugar and cocoa into a bowl. Add the essences and soda to the lukewarm liquid, stir to dissolve, then stir into the dry ingredients with a whisk. Stir in the cool melted fat. Divide the mixture between the 2 sandwich tins and bake for 25 minutes in a fairly hot oven (gas mark 5-6 or 400-425 degrees Fahr.). When cold, sandwich and spread with Vanilla Butter Icing (page 86).

STRAWBERRY CREAM GATEAU

Follow the Special Cake recipe. Turn the mixture into two greased and floured 6½-7½-inch sandwich tins. Bake for 20-25 minutes in the upper part of a moderately hot oven (gas mark 4-5 or 375-400 degrees Fahr.). Turn on to a wire rack to become cold.
For the filling and top of the cake:

1-1½ lb. sweetened fresh or quick-frozen strawberries.
¼-½ pint whipping cream or mock cream (page 45)

While the cake is cooling, gently press half the strawberries, sprinkle them with caster sugar to taste and leave them to become a little juicy. Whip the cream. Add some to the sweetened strawberries and sandwich the layers with the mixture. Pile the remaining cream on top and stud it with the remaining uncrushed berries.

APRICOT OR PEACH CREAM GATEAU

Make as above, substituting sliced stoned apricots or peaches for the strawberries. Sprinkle with lemon juice and a little icing sugar. Peaches should first be skinned. Dip them in boiling water and the skins will slip off easily.

BANANA CREAM GATEAU

Substitute bananas for the strawberries. Slice them, coat with lemon juice to keep them white and sprinkle with icing sugar to taste.

MOCK CREAM

½ tin full cream evaporated milk

2 tablespoons icing sugar

½-1 lemon (juice only)

Pour the evaporated milk into a large bowl. Add the sugar, sifted if necessary, and with a rotary beater whip the milk until it is almost double in bulk. Stir in the strained lemon juice. The cream will not curdle and it will stiffen beautifully. This is a most excellent cream which holds its shape for some time.

DUNDEE CAKE

4 oz. butter or margarine

4 oz. caster sugar

2 large eggs

6 oz. Whitworth's Self-raising Flour

Pinch of salt

12 oz. Whitworth's Dried Fruit Mixture

2 oz. Whitworth's glace cherries

1 oz. Whitworth's blanched halved almonds

Grated rind of half an orange

Grease and flour a 7 in. cake tin. Prepare the oven at a moderate slow heat (gas mark 2 or 325 degrees Fahr.).

Sift the flour and salt. Cream the margarine and sugar. Add the grated orange rind and a heaped tablespoon of the sifted flour, and beat them into the mixture. Add the eggs one at a time, beating the first in well before adding the second. Beat in a portion of the remaining flour, then add the rest in several more portions, mixing well to give a smooth texture and soft dropping consistency, using milk as required. Blend in the fruit.

Transfer the mixture to the tin, and place the halved almonds on the top. Bake about 1¾-2 hours in the middle of the oven, lowering the heat if necessary after about 1½ hours.

GROSVENOR GINGER CAKE

> 8 oz. butter or margarine
> 8 oz. caster sugar
> 4 eggs
> 10 oz. Whitworth's Self-raising Flour
> Pinch of salt
> 6 oz. crystallised ginger, chopped
> Juice of small half lemon
> 2 tablespoons boiling water

Grease and flour a deep square or oblong tin measuring about 10 x 10 in. or 11 x 9 in.

Cream the butter and sugar very well. Beat in the eggs, one at a time, adding a little of the flour to prevent curdling, if necessary. Add half the flour, sifted with the salt, then the chopped ginger. Follow with the remaining flour.

Add the water to the lemon juice and mix into the batter. Turn into the prepared tin, level off and bake for 1-1½ hours in a moderate oven (gas mark 3-4 or 350-375 degrees Fahr.). When cold, cover with a thin coat of glace icing (page 84) and at once decorate with petals of sliced ginger.

★ MARBLE CAKE

> 4 oz. butter or margarine
> 4 oz. caster sugar
> 2 eggs
> 5 oz. Whitworth's Self-raising Flour
> Pinch of salt
> ½ teaspoon vanilla essence
> 2 tablespoons milk
> cochineal
> 1 oz. sweet chocolate melted in 1 dessertspoon hot water

Cream the fat and sugar until very light. Beat in the eggs, one at a time. (If the mixture looks like separating, add a good teaspoon of the flour and go on beating.) Add half the sifted flour and salt and the vanilla essence. Add the remaining flour and milk.

Divide the batter into three portions. Add the cochineal to one, the melted chocolate to another and leave the third as mixed. Place

alternate spoonfuls of the three colours side by side in a greased and floured 6-6½ in. tin. Level off and bake for 45-50 minutes in a moderate oven (gas mark 4-5 or 375-400 degrees Fahr.).
Note.—This is specially good when topped with Chocolate Butter Icing (page 86) and decorated with halved walnuts.

Variation I: **Piebald Cake**
Divide the batter in half. Leave one portion as it is, add 1½ oz. sweet chocolate dissolved in 1½ dessertspoons hot water to the other, then proceed as for Marble Cake.

Variation II: **Two-Tone Layer Cake**
Bake the two batters in *Variation I* in two 6-in. sandwich tins for 20-25 minutes at gas mark 4-5 or 375-400 degrees Fahr. Sandwich with Vanilla, Coffee or Chocolate Butter Icing (page 86).

SNOWDROP CAKE

This cake calls for 3 egg whites. Use the yolks in Buttercup Cake (page 53).

> *2 oz. butter or margarine*
> *2 oz. vegetable fat or other white fat*
> *4 oz. caster sugar*
> *6 oz. Whitworth's Self-raising Flour*
> *Pinch of salt*
> *Milk to mix*
> *½ teaspoon almond essence*
> *3 egg whites*

Grease and flour a 6½-inch cake tin.
Cream the fats together until very soft. Work in the sugar and beat until very light and fluffy. Sift the flour and salt and work about a third into the creamed mixture with the almond essence. Fold in remaining flour in several portions, with one to two tablespoons milk if necessary, to make a fairly firm mixture. Whip the egg whites very stiffly and fold them in.
Bake for 40-45 minutes at gas mark 3-4 or 350–375 deg. Fahr.
When cold, ice with American boiled frosting (page 80), using 1 egg white and spike here and there with little slivers of angelica to simulate the first shoots of snowdrops coming through.

COCONUT RING CAKE

> *4 oz. margarine*
> *4 oz. caster sugar*
> *2 large eggs*
> *6 oz. Whitworth's Self-raising Flour*
> *¼ teaspoon salt*
> *2 oz. Whitworth's desiccated coconut*
> *2 tablespoons milk*

Grease and flour a 7-7½-inch ring mould.

Cream the margarine and sugar until very light. Beat in the eggs, one at a time. Sift the flour and salt and mix in the coconut. Add these dry ingredients to the creamed mixture, alternately with the milk.

Turn into the prepared ring mould and bake for 1-1¼ hours in a moderate oven (gas mark 3-4 or 350-375 degrees Fahr.).

Note.—For a change add, after all other ingredients, 1 oz. each of angelica and glacé cherries cut into thin strips.

MARMALADE CAKE

> *4 oz. butter or margarine*
> *4 oz. caster sugar*
> *2 large eggs*
> *4 tablespoons orange marmalade*
> *1 oz. Whitworth's cut mixed peel*
> *Grated rind of an orange*
> *2 oz. Whitworth's chopped walnuts*
> *10 oz. Whitworth's Self-raising Flour*
> *¼ teaspoon salt*
> *⅓ cup water*

Grease and flour a deep 7-7½-inch cake tin.

Cream the fat and sugar. Beat in the egg yolks until very light. Add and stir in the marmalade, orange peel, grated rind and nuts. Add the sifted flour and salt alternately with the water and beat smooth. Fold in the stiffly beaten egg whites.

Turn into the prepared tin and bake for 1 hour in a moderate oven (gas mark 3-4 or 350-375 degrees Fahr.).

ORANGE PARTY CAKE

7 oz. butter or margarine
7 oz. caster sugar
3 large eggs
8 oz. Whitworth's Self-raising Flour
¼ teaspoon salt
2 tablespoons orange juice
Grated rind of 1 orange
American Frosting (page 80)

Have ready, greased and floured, two 8-8½-inch straight-sided sandwich-tins.

Cream the fat very well, add the sugar and beat until very light. Beat in the eggs, one at a time. (It is a good idea first to sprinkle a little of the flour over the creamed mixture to prevent it from separating.) Add the sifted flour and salt alternately with the orange juice and rind.

Divide the mixture equally between the two tins and bake for 30-35 minutes in the upper half of a moderate oven (gas mark 2-3 or 325-350 degrees Fahr.). A little longer may be required, but listen to the cakes (*see* page 34) and, if there is any sound, return them to the oven for a further few minutes. Turn on to a cake rack to cool.

Icing: Double the quantities for American Frosting (page 80). Halfway towards thickening, add orange essence to taste and, if wished, a few drops of orange culinary colouring. Use some of the icing to sandwich the two layers. Quickly turn the remainder on to the top of the cake and spread it over and down and around the sides in a swirling movement. For a very pretty decoration, peel off thin layers of orange rind, avoiding including any pith. Cover with cold water, bring to the boil and simmer until the peel is tender. Drain and dry. Cut into slender slivers and, before the icing sets, stripe the surface with them to accentuate the swirled icing.

Happy Variations:

Lemon Cake: Follow the above recipe, subsituting lemon juice and grated rind for orange. Flavour the icing with lemon juice.

Tangerine Cake: Use tangerines in the same way.

Speckled Cake: Use 1 oz. less flour than in Orange Cake and lightly mix in 2 oz. grated bar chocolate so that the "specks" will show in the finished cake.

CHOCOLATE CAKE, RICH

8 oz. butter or margarine
8 oz. Whitworth's soft brown sugar
4 oz. black treacle
4 eggs
8 oz. Whitworth's Self-raising Flour
2 oz. cocoa

Grease and flour an 8 in. cake tin. Prepare oven gas mark 3, or 350 degrees Fahr. dropping to 300.

Sieve the flour and cocoa together. Cream the butter, sugar and treacle until soft and light. Gradually beat in the eggs, adding a little of the sieved flour if the mixture shows signs of curdling. Fold in the sieved flour and cocoa.

Transfer into the prepared tin and bake for approx. 1¼ hours.

When cold this cake can be split and sandwiched with Vanilla butter icing (page 86) and if liked the top can be iced with it. Coffee or orange flavoured butter icing is also excellent with chocolate cake.

CHOCOLATE WALNUT CAKE

Layer the above cake with Coffee Butter Icing, to which 1-2 oz. chopped walnuts have been added. Cover with the coffee icing and place quarter walnuts around the edge of the cake.

PARKIN (YORKSHIRE)

½ lb. Whitworth's Self-raising Flour
½ lb. Whitworth's medium oatmeal
¼ teaspoon salt
½-1 teaspoon ground ginger
¼ lb. Whitworth's soft brown sugar
4 oz. lard
½ lb. syrup or black treacle
Under ¼ pint milk

Line a baking-tin measuring about 10 in. x 12 in. with greased greaseproof paper.

Sift the dry ingredients into a basin. Melt together the sugar, fat and syrup or treacle over a low heat. Remove and add the milk. Stir into the dry ingredients. Turn into the lined tin and bake for 1-1¼ hours in a moderately slow oven (gas mark 2 or 325 degrees Fahr.).

Turn on to a wire cake rack. When cold, wrap in greaseproof paper and store in an airtight tin.

GINGERBREAD, OLD-FASHIONED DARK

6 oz. Whitworth's Self-raising Flour
Pinch of salt (optional)
1½ teaspoons ground ginger
1½ teaspoons mixed spice or ground cinnamon
3 oz. margarine
4 oz. golden syrup
4 oz. black treacle
1 egg
2-3 tablespoons milk
½ teaspoon (scant) bicarbonate of soda

Grease and flour a 7 in. x 11 in. tin or a 1½ lb. loaf tin.
Sift the dry ingredients (except the soda) together. Melt together the margarine, syrup and treacle. Cool, then add the egg and beat well. Stir into the dry ingredients. Add up to 2 tablespoons milk. Dissolve the soda in 1 tablespoon milk, stir into the batter and mix well.
Turn into the prepared tin and bake for 40-50 minutes in a moderate oven (gas mark 3-4 or 350-375 degrees Fahr.).
Note.—An easy way to measure the syrup and treacle is to weigh the saucepan, then add the required amounts.

GATEAU ST. HONORE

This is a special Birthday Cake in France, which would be very pleasant for special occasions in this country.
Start with a base of rich short crust pastry (page 8). Roll out to less than ¼ in. thick. Place on a baking sheet. Using a saucepan lid as pattern, cut out a round 7-8 in. in diameter. Remove trimmings. Prick the round all over and bake for 20-25 minutes in a moderately hot oven (gas mark 5-6 or 400-425 degrees Fahr.).
Now make Choux Pastry (page 9). Place in a bag fitted with a ¼-½-inch pipe and pipe small rounds on to a greased baking-sheet to make Profiteroles. Bake as directed on page 16. Fill the Profiteroles with sweetened cream or vanilla-flavoured custard to which you have added a little whipped cream.
Make a syrup with ¼ lb. sugar and 2 tablespoons water. Stir over a low heat until the sugar is dissolved. Bring to the boil without further stirring. After a minute or two, test by dropping a little of the syrup from the tip of a teaspoon into cold water. When it forms a hard ball (248-250 degrees Fahr., if you use a thermometer) it is ready.
Remove and dip the bottom of each Profiterole in the syrup, then stick them close to each other all round the edge of the pastry base. If liked, spoon a little of the syrup over each.

Fill the centre with whipped cream and fruit, or custard enriched with a little more cream, or a good fruit fool, or ice cream beaten at the last minute and topped with fruit.

BATTENBURG CAKE

For this cake, there is a special tin with a division down the centre so that the two mixtures will produce cakes of uniform size. But this cake can be made in two loaf tins.

> *5 oz. butter or margarine*
> *5 oz. caster sugar*
> *2 large eggs*
> *¼ teaspoon salt*
> *8 oz. Whitworth's Self-raising Flour*
> *Vanilla essence to taste*
> *Cochineal or carmine colouring*
> *4-5 tablespoons apricot puree or jam*
> *Almond paste (page 81) or*
> *8 oz. packet Whitworth's marzipan*

Grease and flour 2 loaf tins or use a special Battenburg tin.
Follow the method of making Victoria Sponge Sandwich (page 36). Divide the mixture in half. Put one half in one tin, colour the other to a warm pink and put it in the other tin. Bake for 30-35 minutes in a moderate oven (gas mark 4-5 or 375-400 degrees Fahr.). Turn on to a rack to become cold.
Cut each in half, lengthwise, and trim the 4 pieces so that each strip presents a square end. Spread the sides of two lengths, one pink and one white, with the warmed jam and press the jam sides together. Spread the top with jam. Join the other two pieces in the same way and place them on top—pink over white and white over pink.
Spread three sides of the oblong with more jam. Make ½-¾ lb. almond paste (page 81). Knead and roll it out into a strip which will be long enough and wide enough to wrap around the cake. Place on the cake so that the final join will be underneath, then invert the cake. Spread the former underside (now top) with further jam and bring the two ends of almond paste up and over the cake to join. Press to the cake. Square the corners by gently pressing them with the flat of a knife. Pinch the top corners with the fingers to make a fluted edge. Trim the ends, if necessary.
Wrap in waxed paper and leave for several hours before cutting.

CHERRY CAKE

8 oz. Whitworth's Self-raising Flour
Pinch of salt
4 oz. (20 to 25) Whitworth's glacé cherries
4 oz. margarine or butter
4 oz. caster sugar
1 egg
Milk to mix

Grease and flour a 6-inch cake tin. Set the oven for moderate heat (350 degrees Fahr. or gas mark 3).
Sift the flour and salt together. Halve the cherries and, if desired, dust them with a little of the flour. Rub the fat into the flour to the fine breadcrumb stage. Mix in the sugar. Stir in the beaten egg and enough milk to produce a batter of fairly stiff consistency (about 3 to 4 tablespoons, depending on the size of the egg). Stir the mixture very well until quite smooth. Stir in the cherries.
Turn into the prepared tin and bake for 1¼ hours, lowering the heat towards the end, if necessary.
Note. — For a 7 to 7½-inch tin, double the above quantities and increase the baking time by 25 to 30 minutes.
This cake does not need to be iced but, for special occasions, it can be. For the icing, use American Frosting. Before it is set, decorate with a cluster of cherries made with halved glacé cherries with stems and leaves of angelica.

BUTTERCUP CAKE

This cake calls for 3 egg yolks. Use the 3 whites in Snowdrop Cake (page 47).

3 oz. butter or margarine
3 oz. caster sugar
3 egg yolks
6 oz. Whitworth's Self-raising Flour
Pinch of salt
Milk to mix
¼ teaspoon vanilla essence

Grease and flour a 7-inch cake tin.
Cream the fat and sugar until very light and fluffy. Beat in the yolks, one at a time. Sift the flour and salt and fold into the mixture with the essence, using two to three tablespoons milk to give a fairly firm mixture. Bake for ¾-1 hour in a moderate oven (gas mark 3-4 or 350-375 degrees Fahr.).
When cold, ice with butter icing (page 86) tinted a warm butter colour with egg colouring.

BOILED FRUIT CAKE OR FRUIT CAKE, EGGLESS

8 oz. Whitworth's Self-raising Flour
4 oz. butter
4 oz. sugar
6 oz. Whitworth's Dried Fruit Mixture
¼ pint water
Pinch of salt
1 level teaspoon mixed spice
½ level teaspoon grated nutmeg

Prepare the oven at a moderate heat, approximately 325 degrees Fahr. or gas mark 2. Place butter, sugar, mixed fruit, and water, in a saucepan, bring slowly to the boil and continue boiling gently for about 5 minutes. Remove from flame and leave to stand while carrying out the following operations. Grease and flour a 6 inch cake tin, weigh out the flour and sift together with the salt and spices into a basin. By this time the boiled mixture will have lost its first heat. Pour it, while still quite hot, into the flour mixture, stir well, and put into the cake tin. Bake for 1¼ hours.

This cake keeps moist for a long while.

SULTANA NUT CAKE

8 oz. Whitworth's Self-raising Flour
Pinch of salt
6 oz. butter
6 oz. caster sugar
4 oz. Whitworth's sultanas
2 oz. Whitworth's desiccated coconut
2 eggs
Milk to mix

Cream the butter and sugar together until soft, beat in the eggs one at a time. Stir in the sifted flour, salt, sultanas, coconut and milk if needed to make a fairly soft consistency. Pour into a greased 7 inch cake tin and bake at 350 degrees Fahr., or gas mark 3 for about 1¼ hours.

Note. — This mixture makes tasty small cakes, baked in bun tins for about 20 minutes at 375 degrees Fahr. or gas mark 4.

BOILED FRUIT CAKE WITH EGG

8 oz. Whitworth's washed sultanas
¼ pint water
4 oz. Whitworth's soft brown sugar
4 oz. butter or margarine
9 oz. Whitworth's Self-raising Flour
2 level teaspoons mixed spice
Pinch of salt
1 egg

Place sultanas, fat, sugar, and water, in a saucepan. Bring to the boil and allow to simmer gently for five minutes. Remove from heat and allow to stand while the following operations are carried out:—
Grease and flour a six-inch cake tin. Prepare the oven for a moderate heat (gas mark 3 or 350 degrees Fahr.). Sift the dry ingredients together. Now stir the fairly hot liquid ingredients into the dry mixture, and add the egg. Mix to form a fairly smooth batter, place in the tin, and bake for one-and-a-quarter to one-and-a-half hours, reducing the heat if necessary after about an hour.

CURRANT FLAPJACKS

8 oz. breakfast oats
Pinch of salt
5 oz. butter
3 oz. Whitworth's demerara sugar
2 oz. golden syrup
4 oz. Whitworth's currants
Squeeze lemon juice

Melt the butter, sugar and syrup slowly in a saucepan. Stir in the oats, salt, currants and lemon juice. Press the mixture into a greased Yorkshire pudding tin. Bake at 325 degrees Fahr. or gas mark 2 for 30 minutes. When slightly cool, mark off the flapjacks in fingers and remove from the tin when cold.

SMALL CAKES

"BUTTERFLIES"

> 3 oz. butter or margarine
> 3 oz. caster sugar
> ¼ teaspoon vanilla essence
> 1 egg
> 4 oz. Whitworth's Self-raising Flour
> Pinch of salt
> Milk to mix
> Mock cream

Grease and flour 9-12 small cup-cake tins.

Cream the fat and sugar. Beat in the essence and egg. Fold in half the sifted flour and salt, then add a little milk and the remaining flour. The batter should be fairly soft. Two-thirds fill the tins and bake for 20-25 minutes in a moderate oven (gas mark 4 or 375 degrees Fahr.). When nicely browned, turn on to a wire rack to cool.

To shape the "Butterflies": cut a thin slice off the top of each cake and cut in half. Pipe slightly sweetened whipped cream on each side of the cut top of each cake and prop the halved slices on it to make "wings". Pipe a slender "body" over the joins.

CUP CAKES (ICED)

Bake the Butterfly Cake mixture in small paper cases. When cold, pour on each a little Chocolate Glacé Icing (page 84) or plain white Glacé Icing (page 84).

QUEEN CAKES

To the Butterfly Cake mixture, add 2 oz. Whitworth's currants and the grated rind of a small lemon.

ROSEBERY CAKES

To the Butterfly Cake mixture, add 1 oz. Whitworth's ground almonds and 1-2 oz. chopped glacé cherries.

For CHOCOLATE BUTTERFLIES,

use 1 oz. cocoa and 3 oz. Whitworth's Self-raising Flour.

MADELEINES

> *2 eggs*
> *Same weight (as eggs) in caster sugar*
> *Same weight in Whitworth's Self-raising Flour*
> *Same weight in butter*
> *Pinch of salt*
> *Raspberry or red currant jelly*
> *Whitworth's desiccated coconut*
> *Whitworth's glacé cherries*
> *Angelica*

Beat the eggs and sugar until very light. Stir in the sifted flour and salt, a little at a time. Finally, stir in the melted—not hot—butter.

Have ready small dariole moulds, thickly greased and floured. Two-thirds fill them with the mixture. Bake for 20 minutes in a moderate oven (gas mark 3 or 350 degrees Fahr.). Turn on to a wire rack and, when cold, level off the tops, if necessary, then spread the sides and the narrower ends with jelly and roll in the desiccated coconut. Place a cherry and two tiny "leaves" of angelica on top of each cake, with a little of the jelly to make them stick.

Note.—French Madeleines are baked in little shell-shaped tins.

VIENNESE TARTS

> *4 oz. Whitworth's Self-raising Flour*
> *4 oz. Whitworth's Plain Flour*
> *7 oz. butter*
> *2 oz. caster sugar*
> *Vanilla essence to taste*

Sift the flours together. Cream the butter and sugar until smooth. Add half the flour mixture and the essence and beat until nice and light. Add remaining flours and beat until light and smooth.

With a large rose pipe, pipe the mixture in swirls into small paper cases, filling them to the top, then bake for 15-20 minutes in a moderate oven (gas mark 3 or 350 degrees Fahr.). Leave to become cold, then place a dab of jam on each tart and pipe whipped cream on top, if liked.

DATE DUMPIES

4 oz. margarine

3 oz. caster sugar

1 egg

8 oz. Whitworth's Self-raising Flour

Pinch of salt

Very little milk

Stoned dates

Cream the fat and sugar until light. Beat in the egg. Mix in the flour, sifted with the salt, and enough milk to make a dough a little softer than short crust consistency. Pinch off walnut-sized pieces and flatten them in the palms of the hands. Wrap each around a stoned date. Place, joined side down, on a greased baking sheet and bake for 15-20 minutes in a fairly hot oven (gas mark 6 or 425 degrees Fahr.).

Variation I:
Fill the cavity of each date with a piece of crystallised ginger.

Variation II:
Omit 1 oz. flour and substitute 1 oz. cocoa. Fill the cavity of each date with half a walnut or a pellet of marzipan.

JAP CAKES

As these cakes are suggested as one of the ways of using egg whites when only the yolks are required in a recipe, here are the proportions rather than the actual amounts. If, therefore, you have two, three or four egg whites, you can double, treble or quadruple the quantities.

1 egg white

2 oz. Whitworth's ground almonds

2 oz. caster sugar

A drop of almond essence

Coffee or Vanilla Butter Icing (page 86)

Line a shallow tin with greaseproof paper brushed with oil.

Whip the egg white stiffly. Fold in the ground almonds and sugar and add the essence. Spread ¼ in. thick in the tin and bake in a moderately slow oven (gas mark 2 or 325 degrees Fahr.) until almost set approx. 20 minutes. Remove and stamp into 1½-inch rounds. Return to the oven and bake until quite firm.

Take out and remove the rounds only and place them on a rack to cool. Return the trimmings to the oven to become a really golden tone. When cold, roll into crumbs with a rolling-pin.

Spread half the cakes with coffee or vanilla butter icing and gently press the remaining half on top. Spread the tops and sides with butter icing and coat them with the crumbs. Garnish the top, if liked, with a dot of glacé icing in the centre.

DATE STICKS

> *1 egg*
> *1 oz. caster sugar*
> *Pinch of salt*
> *1 dessertspoon melted margarine*
> *½-¾ lb. chopped dates*
> *1-2 tablespoons Whitworth's chopped walnuts (optional)*
> *3 oz. Whitworth's Self-raising Flour*
> *1 dessertspoon hot water*

Beat together the egg, sugar, salt and margarine. Add the dates, and if liked, nuts. Add, alternately the flour and hot water.

Spread the mixture in a greased and floured shallow tin, about 8 in x 9 in. Bake for 20-25 minutes in a moderately hot oven (gas mark 4-5 or 375-400 degrees Fahr.). Remove, cut into fingers and place on a wire rack to cool. Roll in a little caster sugar, if liked.

Note. —If desired, add up to 1 oz. Whitworth's chopped mixed peel.

★ CHOCOLATE NUT FINGERS

> *2 oz. plain chocolate*
> *3 oz. butter or margarine*
> *4 oz. caster sugar*
> *2 eggs*
> *Pinch of salt*
> *2 oz. Whitworth's Self-raising Flour*
> *2 oz. chopped Whitworth's almonds, or walnuts*
> *½ teaspoon vanilla essence*

Melt the chocolate in a basin over boiling water then add the butter and melt it. Remove and cool, but keep soft. Beat in the sugar, eggs (one at a time) and salt. Add the flour, nuts and vanilla essence.

Spread on a well-greased and floured tin, about 8 in. square, and bake for 1 hour in a moderately slow oven (gas mark 2-3 or 325-350 degrees Fahr.). Cut into fingers.

Variation:
Add ¾ teacup chopped dates or halved Whitworth's sultanas. Bake a little longer.

★ *Basic Recipe*   59

FAIRY CAKES

> 4 oz. margarine
> 4 oz. caster sugar
> 2 eggs
> 6 oz. Whitworth's Self-raising Flour
> Pinch of salt
> 2-3 oz. Whitworth's currants or 1½ oz. Whitworth's
>   glace cherries (chopped)
> ½ oz. Whitworth's ground almonds

Cream the margarine and sugar until light and fluffy. Whisk in the beaten eggs. Add the sifted flour and salt, currants and nuts.

Turn into greased and floured Queen Cake tins or paper cases and bake for 16-18 minutes in a moderately hot oven (gas mark 5-6 or 400-425 degrees Fahr.).

Note.—One shell egg and 2 tablespoons water can be used in place of 2 shell eggs.

ROCK CAKES

> 8 oz. Whitworth's Self-raising Flour
> ¼ teaspoon salt
> ¼ teaspoon mixed spice
> 2 oz. caster sugar
> 2 oz. margarine or dripping
> 2½ oz. Whitworth's Dried Fruit Mixture
> 1 egg
> A little milk

Grease 2 baking sheets.

Sift together the first 4 ingredients. Rub in the fat, then add the fruit. Beat the egg and mix mixture with enough milk to make a very stiff mixture.

Place in 12-14 heaps on the baking sheets and roughen them with a fork. Bake for 15-20 minutes in a fairly hot oven (gas mark 4-5 or 375-400 degrees Fahr.).

★ MOCHA CAKES

> *3 oz. margarine*
> *3 oz. caster sugar*
> *2 eggs*
> *5 oz. Whitworth's Self-raising Flour*
> *Pinch of salt*
> *1 tablespoon warm water (about)*

Blend the fat and sugar until very light and creamy. Beat in the eggs, one at a time. Add the sifted flour and salt, then, at the last minute, add the warm water.

Turn into a well greased and floured Yorkshire Pudding tin, about 7 in x 9 in., and bake for 20 minutes in a moderate oven (gas mark 4 or 375 degrees Fahr.), and then for a further 5 minutes at gas mark 5 or 400 degrees Fahr. Turn out and, when cold, store until next day.

Cut into small squares or diamonds, spread with Vanilla Butter Icing (page 86) and roll in chopped roasted blanched almonds.

Variation I:
Spread with coffee-flavoured Butter Icing, then roll in chopped almonds or chopped walnuts.

Variation II:
Spread with the Butter Icing and place a piece of glacé cherry and a small strip of angelica on top of each cake.

HERMITS

> *1 oz. butter or margarine*
> *4 oz. caster sugar*
> *1 large egg*
> *4 oz. chopped Whitworth's stoned raisins*
> *2 oz. chopped Whitworth's walnuts*
> *5 oz. Whitworth's Self-raising Flour*
> *Pinch of salt*
> *Pinch of cinnamon*
> *Tip of teaspoon grated nutmeg*

Cream the fat and sugar. Add the beaten egg, raisins and nuts. Beat well together. Sift the flour, salt and spices and add to make a stiff mixture. Drop spoonfuls on to a greased and floured baking sheet, allowing for spreading, and bake for 15 minutes in a moderately hot oven (gas mark 5 or 400 degrees Fahr.).

★ *Basic Recipe*

JUNE ROSES CAKES

Victoria Sponge (page 36) or Genoese (page 69)
Apricot puree or jam (sieved)
Almond paste (page 81)
Carmine colouring
Whitworth's desiccated coconut

Make the cake and bake it in a shallow 8-9 inch tin so that there will be a slab about 1¼-1½ in. deep. Leave for 24 hours then cut into 1½-2-inch rounds. Make the almond paste and tint it a soft pink with a little carmine colouring. If the paste is a little on the firm side, add a drop or two of water to make it slightly more pliable. Roll out very thin between wax paper so that it can be handled easily and stamp into plain small rounds, about three-quarters of the diameter of the cakes.

Spread the apricot puree or jam on the top and sides of the cakes and roll only the sides in the coconut. Now take the almond paste rounds and pinch each at one end to shape into petals. Place on the cake, pressing gently on the apricot puree. Repeat, slightly overlapping the rounds, allowing five for each cake, so that they fall like petals.

In the centre, place a silver ball or a yellow mimosa one.

TUCK-BOX BUNS

4 oz. butter or margarine
6 oz. caster sugar
1 egg
1 tablespoon syrup
12 oz. Whitworth's Self-raising Flour
¼ teaspoon salt
6 oz. Whitworth's Dried Fruit Mixture
Milk to mix (approx. ¼ pint)

Cream the fat. Work in the sugar, then beat in the egg and syrup very well. Add a quarter of the sifted flour and salt, then the fruit. Add the milk and remaining flour, a little of each at a time, until the mixture is of a good dropping consistency.

Divide into greased patty tins and bake for about 20 minutes in a fairly hot oven (gas mark 5-6 or 400-425 degrees Fahr.).

Variation: **Tuck-Box Cake**

Turn whole mixture into a greased and floured tin, 7 in x 3½ in., and bake for 1½ to 1¾ hours in a moderate oven (gas mark 3-4 or 350-375 degrees Fahr.).

SPECIAL CAKES for SPECIAL OCCASIONS

CHRISTMAS CAKE

As rich cakes mature with keeping, it is well to make this Christmas Cake at least a fortnight in advance.

> *8 oz. butter or margarine*
> *8 oz. Whitworth's soft brown sugar or caster sugar*
> *1 tablespoon black treacle or golden syrup*
> *4 large eggs*
> *3-4 tablespoons sherry or strained cold tea*
> *½ teaspoon vanilla essence*
> *4 oz. Whitworth's Self-raising Flour*
> *6 oz. Whitworth's Plain Flour*
> *¼ teaspoon salt*
> *½ teaspoon mixed spice*
> *Pinch ground cinnamon*
> *Pinch grated nutmeg*
> *12 oz. Whitworth's currants*
> *12 oz. Whitworth's sultanas (half of them chopped)*
> *6 oz. Whitworth's stoned raisins or Whitworth's seedless raisins*
> *2 oz. Whitworth's chopped peel*
> *2 oz. Whitworth's ground almonds*
> *2 oz. Whitworth's glacé cherries, quartered*
> *Grated rind of 1 small lemon*

Grease and flour an 8-9-inch cake tin or line it with two thicknesses of greaseproof paper.

Cream the fat and sugar together. Beat in the treacle.

Beat the eggs, sherry (or tea) and vanilla essence together and mix them in, alternating with the flours, sifted with the salt and spices. (If spices are not liked, they can be omitted without affecting the cake.) Add the remaining ingredients, but do not over-mix.

(If you have an electric mixer, use it only to cream the fat and sugar and mix in the other ingredients by hand, as the mixture must not be overbeaten.)

The mixture should be fairly stiff so that, when a spoonful is taken up, it will fall when a little jerk is given to it.

Turn into the prepared tin and level off. Leave to rest for 10 minutes, then give the tin a gentle tap on the table to settle the mixture.

Bake for 3¾-4¼ hours just below the centre of a slow oven (gas mark 1 or 275-300 degrees Fahr.), but test after 4 hours (see page 34) when the cake may be sufficiently baked. In some ovens, it may require longer. This cake has been tested at various temperatures and the one given produces the best all-round results in a modern cooker—a moist enough but thoroughly baked cake, with very thin crust all round.

Leave the cake to cool in the tin, after which it can be gently turned out on to a cake rack without danger of it breaking.

Leave for at least a day before putting the cake in a tin, to make quite sure that it is cold all through, then leave for several days before coating with almond paste (page 81). After that, leave for at least a week before icing with Royal Icing (page 82).

Note.—In the Xmas Cake recipe given above, two and a half 12 oz. packets of Whitworth's Dried Fruit Mixture may be used instead of the dried fruits and chopped peel.

VARIOUS SIZES OF CHRISTMAS CAKE

For a 6-7-inch cake halve the above ingredients. Bake as above for 3-3½ hours, but test after 3 hours.

For a 9-inch cake, add a quarter more of the listed ingredients and bake as above for 6-6½ hours, testing after 6 hours.

For a 10-11-inch cake, double the ingredients and bake as above for 7-7½ hours, testing after 7 hours.

For the Almond Paste and Royal Icing for these cakes, see pages 81 and 82.

SIMNEL CAKE

The quantities here are for a cake measuring 8-8½ inches in diameter. First, make the almond paste.

> *8 oz. caster sugar*
> *8 oz. icing sugar*
> *1 lb. Whitworth's ground almonds*
> *2 small eggs*
> *A few drops almond essence*
> *1 teaspoon sherry or brandy*
> *Lemon juice as required*

Sieve the sugars and ground almonds into a basin. Stir in the lightly beaten eggs, almond essence, sherry or brandy and lemon juice to make a pliable, easy-to-handle "dough". Knead just enough to smooth out any joins. Do not over-knead, as this would make the paste oily.

64

Cut off a third of the almond paste for the filling. Form it into a ball, then, using the tin as a pattern, roll out to a round slightly smaller than the diameter of the tin. Wrap the remaining paste in greaseproof paper and set it aside for the top of the cake.

For the cake:

> *6 oz. butter or margarine*
> *6 oz. caster sugar*
> *6 oz. Whitworth's Self-raising Flour*
> *2 oz. Whitworth's Plain Flour*
> *4 eggs*
> *½ teaspoon salt*
> *½ teaspoon mixed spice*
> *8 oz. Whitworth's currants*
> *8 oz. Whitworth's sultanas*
> *4 oz. Whitworth's seedless raisins*
> *1½ oz. chopped Whitworth's almonds*
> *3 oz. quartered Whitworth's glacé cherries*
> *3 oz. Whitworth's chopped mixed peel*
> *Grated rind of ½ lemon*
> *A few drops almond essence*

Grease the 8-8½-inch cake tin and line it with 2-3 thicknesses of greaseproof paper.

Cream the fat. Work in the sugar and beat well. Sift the flours, salt and spice together. Mix in the eggs, one at a time, alternating with the flour mixture. Finally, add and work in the remaining ingredients.

Turn half the mixture into the prepared tin and level off. Place the round of almond paste on top, then add the remaining mixture and level off.

Bake in a moderately slow oven (gas mark 2 or 325 degrees Fahr.) for up to 4½ hours, but test the cake after 4 hours. (See notes of page 34.) When the cake is cold, divide the remaining almond paste in half. Roll out one portion to fit the top of the cake. Brush the top of the cake with white of egg and place the almond paste firmly in position. Trim the sides then slip the cake under the grill to give the paste a delicate brown colour. Form the remaining paste into 11 little balls of uniform size and toast them, too.

Make 11 dots of icing around the top of the cake and place the almond paste balls on them. Decorate with little chicks or other Easter ornaments.

Note. —Halve the ingredients for a 6-6½-inch cake.

SPONGE CAKE (FATLESS)
MIXTURES

These are the mixtures for Swiss Rolls and, because there is no fat in
them, for sandwich cakes where very rich butter or cream fillings are
used. Also, because they are fatless, they make excellent cakes for
children's parties.

Use these mixtures, too, for making small sponge cakes or fingers for
trifles and sweets of the Charlotte Russe type.

★ SPONGE MIXTURE I

> *2 eggs*
> *3 oz. caster sugar*
> *1 tablespoon warm water*
> *3 oz. Whitworth's Self-raising Flour*
> *Pinch of salt*

Whip the eggs for 3-4 minutes. Add the sugar and whip again for 5
minutes. Add the water and fold in the flour, sifted with the salt, to
incorporate it but with as little mixing as possible. Turn into the
prepared tin and bake as directed. (See following recipes.)

★ *Basic Recipe*

★ SPONGE MIXTURE II

This is a very light and special sponge mixture to be used for special occasions.

> *3 eggs*
> *3 oz. caster sugar*
> *Pinch of salt*
> *3 oz. Whitworth's Self-raising Flour*

Whip the egg whites until stiff but not dry. Add the yolks and whip until evenly mixed. Add the sugar and salt and whip until the mixture is thick. Sprinkle the flour over the top and gently fold it in, making sure that all is well mixed, but do not over-mix.

Use in the following recipes in the same way as for Sponge Mixture I.

SWISS ROLL

Before starting to mix the cake, line a greased 9 in x 12 in. Swiss Roll tin with greased greaseproof paper, greased side up. Let the paper be slightly larger than the tin. Make a cut in each corner so that they can be turned to make them square when fitted into the tin. Or, if the oven bakes better without the paper, simply grease and flour the tin.

Turn the mixture into the tin and spread it well to the sides, having slightly less in the centre. Bake for 7-9 minutes in a hot oven (gas mark 6-7 or 425-450 degrees Fahr.), according to the temperature. Do not be afraid to remove it from the oven after 7 minutes, for it will probably be baked then. If it is left until it has a firm crust, it will crack when it is rolled.

Meanwhile, have 2-3 tablespoons of jam warming. Wring a tea towel out in warm water and spread out. On it, place a piece of greaseproof paper sprinkled with caster sugar. Turn the Swiss Roll and tin on to it, lift off the tin at once and peel off the paper. Immediately trim the edges with a sharp knife, spread the jam not quite to the edges and turn in one end fairly firmly. With the assistance of the sugared paper, roll up the cake and leave it to rest firmly on the join.

SPONGE SANDWICH

Grease and flour two 7-inch sandwich tins. Divide the mixture evenly between them. Bake for 15-17 minutes in the top of a moderately hot oven (gas mark 5 or 400 degrees Fahr.). At once turn on to sugared paper to help to keep their shape. When cold, sandwich with butter icing (page 86), whipped sweetened cream and raspberry jam or simply jam.

★ *Basic Recipe*

SPONGE CAKE (DEEP)

Grease a deep 6-6½-inch cake tin and coat the inside with a teaspoon of flour and one of caster sugar, sifted together. Turn the mixture into it and bake for 45 minutes in a moderate oven (gas mark 3 or 350 degrees Fahr.).

SPONGE FLAN

For this, there are special tins, ranging from small to large, which produce a baked flan with a depression in the centre which one can fill with fruit and cream or fruit and ice cream or anything one wishes.
Grease and flour a tin 7½ in.-8 in. in diameter. Turn the sponge mixture into it and bake for 10-12 minutes in the top of a moderately hot oven (gas mark 6 or 425 degrees Fahr.). Turn on to sugared paper and, when cold, fill as desired.

SPONGE FINGERS

Grease sponge-finger tins and dust them with flour and caster sugar (half and half). Spoon or pipe the mixture into them until fairly full. Sprinkle with caster sugar. Bake for 7-10 minutes in a moderately hot oven (gas mark 6 or 425 degrees Fahr.).

SPONGE CAKES (SMALL)

Proceed as for Sponge Fingers, using small sponge cake tins and baking for 9—10 minutes.

LEMON-DATE FILLING

Prepare a Victoria Sandwich and put the layers together with this filling: mix 1 teacup of sugar with 3 tablespoons flour: add ½ teacup water. Cook in a double saucepan, stirring constantly, until thick. Add 2 tablespoon lemon juice, a little grated lemon rind, 1 tablespoon butter or margarine and 1 teacup dates, stoned and chopped. A handful of chopped walnuts makes it even nicer. Cool the mixture before spreading it between the layers.

GENOESE SPONGE

This is the aristocrat of the sponge cake mixture, to which oiled butter is added. Oiled butter is simply butter melted at a very low heat, left for a few minutes then poured off, leaving the milky residue behind. For the cake mixture, the butter should be liquid but cool.

Have ready greased a 7-inch tin with, on the bottom, a round of greased greaseproof paper, greased side up. Or line a Swiss Roll tin with greased greaseproof paper.

> *3 large eggs or 4 small ones*
> *4 oz. (scant) caster sugar*
> *3 oz. oiled butter*
> *3 oz. Whitworth's Self-raising Flour*

Break the eggs into a basin, add the sugar and just mix together. Place over a pan of hot water, without the basin touching the water. The water must not boil because that would tend to cook the mixture instead of helping to thicken it. Whip with a wire whisk for 5-10 minutes or until the whisk leaves a trail which does not at once run together. The mixture should be quite thick and increased in bulk.

Remove to the table and whisk for another 5 minutes or so until the mixture is cool. Lightly fold in half the liquid butter. Sprinkle half the flour over the surface and very lightly fold it in, over and over. Add the remaining butter and flour in the same way. This mixture must not be overworked.

Turn into the prepared tin. Bake the round one for 40-45 minutes in a moderate oven (gas mark 4 or 375 degrees Fahr.) or the shallow one for 15-20 minutes at a slightly higher temperature.

This cake can be iced, or the round cake can be split through in half, sandwiched with any favourite filling and then iced. When baked in a Swiss Roll tin, the sponge can be cut into small cakes and iced all over. In this case, bake the cake the day before you cut it so that the crumb will not so easily become detached when the icing is being applied.

CHOCOLATE SWISS ROLL

> *2 eggs*
> *4 oz. caster sugar*
> *3 oz. Whitworth's Self-raising Flour*
> *1 level tablespoon cocoa*
> *1-1½ tablespoons warm water*
> *Vanilla butter icing (page 86)*

Follow the method for Sponge Mixture I, adding the cocoa with the flour. Then, without any filling, roll up with the sugared paper inside. When cold, unroll, spread with the butter icing and roll up again.

WONDERFUL THINGS TO HAVE ON HAND—

HOME-MADE BISCUITS

Biscuits are so easy and quick to make, so much in demand for tea, elevenses and with good-night drinks. Why not make a speciality of them? With one or two basic recipes as starting points, you can ring countless changes. Indeed, from one batch of dough you can make several sorts of delicious biscuits in the one baking.

Remember that the very name—biscuits—means twice-cooked, and indicates the crispness which is the first essential of good biscuits.

RULES FOR CRISPNESS

Rub the fat well into the dry ingredients or cream the fat and sugar well together according to directions.

Roll out the mixture as thinly as possible but don't over-flour the board—this will make your biscuits streaky. It is a good idea to roll out biscuit dough between sheets of greaseproof paper.

Bake carefully in a *moderate* oven, till evenly coloured. Burned biscuits are most unattractive, but there must be heat enough to set the dough.

After baking, allow biscuits to cool completely. Then store at once in an air-tight tin.

70

★ SUGAR BISCUITS

> *8 oz. Whitworth's Self-raising Flour*
> *Pinch of salt*
> *3-4 oz. butter or margarine*
> *3-4 oz. caster sugar*
> *1 small egg or 1 large egg yolk*

Sift the flour and salt into a bowl. Rub in the fat, then work in the sugar. Add the beaten egg (or egg yolk) and knead very well together. Roll out to one-eighth inch thick and cut into fancy rounds. Brush with a little beaten egg and sprinkle with sugar. Bake for 10-15 minutes in a moderate oven (gas mark 3-4 or 350-375 degrees Fahr.).

Variations ad infinitum . . .

Almond-Apricot Sandwich Biscuits

Work together two tablespoons each of ground almonds and apricot jam. Sandwich the biscuits with the mixture.

Chocolate Biscuits

On each biscuit as it comes from the oven, put a little grated bar chocolate and, as it melts, spread it with a knife.

Easter Biscuits

To the basic mixture, add 2-3 oz. Whitworth's currants, ½ teaspoon mixed spice and a little grated nutmeg. Decorate some biscuits with glacé cherries and angelica, others with "hundreds and thousands".

Lemon Biscuits

Use the basic mixture, but add the grated rind of a lemon to the dry ingredients before mixing. Press a piece of candied lemon peel on each biscuit before baking.

★ *Basic Recipe*

71

Spicy Seed Biscuits.
Add a good teaspoon of caraway seeds and ½ teaspoon ground cinnamon to the dry ingredients and bake as usual.

MACAROONS

> ½ lb. caster or granulated sugar
> ¼ lb. Whitworth's ground almonds
> 2 whites of eggs
> A few drops of almond or vanilla essence
> 2 teaspoons Whitworth's ground rice
> Whitworth's split blanched almonds

Stir the sugar, ground almonds and egg whites together for 8-10 minutes. Work in the ground rice and essence. If the mixture seems a little too firm, add up to ½ teaspoon water. Have ready small squares of rice or wafer paper on baking sheets. Drop small teaspoons of the mixture on the centre of each (or on greased and floured sheets) and press a split blanched almond on each. Bake for 20-25 minutes in a moderate oven (gas mark 3 or 350 degrees Fahr.).

Variation: **Mock Macaroons**
Beat the egg whites until stiff. Fold in the sugar, 2 oz. crushed Weetabix, ½ oz. flour and a few drops of almond essence. Bake as above.

DIGESTIVE BISCUITS

> 3 oz. Whitworth's medium oatmeal
> 5 oz. Whitworth's Self-raising Flour
> Pinch of bicarbonate of soda
> ¼ teaspoon salt
> 1½ oz. sugar
> 4 oz. margarine or butter
> 1½ teaspoons milk or water

Mix the dry ingredients. Rub in the fat. Add just enough liquid to bind. Knead very well. *Avoid adding any more liquid.* Roll out to less than ¼ in. thick, cut into rounds and bake for 15 minutes in a moderate oven (gas mark 3 or 350 degrees Fahr.).

GINGER SNAPS

> 2 oz. margarine, lard or dripping
> 2 tablespoons golden syrup
> 4 oz. Whitworth's Self-raising Flour
> 1 dessertspoon caster sugar
> 1 rounded teaspoon ground ginger
> ½ level teaspoon ground cinnamon
> ½ teaspoon bicarbonate of soda

Have ready-greased 2-3 baking sheets.
Melt the fat and syrup together. Sift the remaining ingredients into a bowl and stir the slightly cooled fat and syrup into them. Form into small balls between the palms of the hands and drop these on the baking sheets, leaving space for them to spread.
Bake for 15-18 minutes in a moderate oven (gas mark 3 or 350 degrees Fahr.).

★ COOKIES

> 3 oz. margarine or butter
> 3 oz. caster sugar
> 1 good tablespoon golden syrup
> ½ teaspoon vanilla essence
> Pinch of bicarbonate of soda
> 2 tablespoons hot water
> 3 oz. Whitworth's Self-raising Flour
> 7-8 oz. breakfast oats
> Pinch of salt

Cream the fat and sugar. Beat in the syrup and essence until light. Mix the soda and water and beat in. Fold in the sifted flour, breakfast oats and salt.
Grease 3 baking sheets. Drop teaspoonfuls of the mixture on to them, well apart, and bake for 15 minutes in a moderate slow oven (gas mark 2-3 or 325-350 degrees Fahr.).

Variation I: **Coconut Cookies**

Use Whitworth's desiccated coconut in place of half the breakfast oats.

Variation II: **Mum's Cookies**

In place of rolled oats, use 5-6 oz. crushed Weetabix.
★ *Basic Recipe*

73

BRANDY SNAPS

> 3 oz. butter or margarine
> 3 oz. golden syrup
> 3 oz. caster sugar
> 3 oz. Whitworth's self-raising Flour
> 1 teaspoon ground ginger
> 1 teaspoon vanilla essence

Melt the fat, syrup and sugar in a pan large enough to hold all the ingredients. Do not overheat. Stir in the flour and ginger, sifted together, and the essence.

Drop teaspoonfuls, well apart, on to the greased baking sheets and bake for 8-10 minutes in a moderate oven (gas mark 3 or 350 degrees Fahr.). Lift off with a knife and, while hot, roll round the handle of a wooden spoon.

Variation I: **Walnut Brandy Snaps**

Add 2 oz. chopped walnuts to above recipe.

Variation II: **Almond Brandy Snaps**

Use chopped almonds instead of walnuts.

GARIBALDI BISCUITS

> 2 oz. Whitworth's currants or Eccles Cake filling (page 13)
> 1½ oz. butter or margarine
> 4 oz. Whitworth's Self-raising Flour
> Pinch of salt
> 1 oz. caster sugar
> Milk to mix
> White of egg or milk
> Caster sugar

Rub the butter into the sifted flour and salt. Add the sugar and enough milk to make a pliable dough. Roll out very thinly, keeping the sides and ends as straight as possible. Sprinkle the currants over one half of the dough, fold the other half over and again roll out to less than ¼ in. thick. Place on a greased baking sheet. Cut through into small squares and brush with white of egg or milk and sprinkle with caster sugar. Bake for 15 minutes to a golden brown in a fairly hot oven (gas mark 6 or 425 degrees Fahr.).

SHORTBREAD

5 oz. butter or margarine
7 oz. Whitworth's Self-raising Flour
1 oz. rice flour (or Whitworth's ground rice)
Pinch of salt
3 oz. caster sugar

Cream the fat very well and gradually work the sifted dry ingredients into it. Knead into a pliable mixture and divide in two. Flatten out into two ½ in. thick cakes and pinch the edges to make a fluted rim. Place on a baking sheet and prick with a fork into wedge shapes. Bake for 40 minutes in a moderately slow oven (gas mark 2-3 or 325-350 degrees Fahr.). Cool on a wire rack and store in a tin.

ALMOND SHORTBREAD BISCUITS

10-12 oz. Whitworth's Self-raising Flour
¼ teaspoon salt
8 oz. caster sugar
1 cup finely chopped Whitworth's blanched almonds
8 oz. butter or margarine

Knead the flour, salt, sugar and almonds into the fat. Pinch off small pieces and mould them into flat round cakes in the palms of the hands. Place on a baking sheet, allow room for spreading and press a split almond on each. Bake for 20-25 minutes in a moderate oven (gas mark 3 or 350 degrees Fahr.).

SEMOLINA SHORTBREAD BISCUITS

5 oz. butter or margarine
3 oz. Whitworth's Self-raising Flour
4 oz. Whitworth's semolina
2 oz. caster sugar
Pinch of salt

Cream the fat very well. Gradually work in the sifted dry ingredients. Knead well together. Roll out to ¼ in. thick and stamp into rounds with a cutter. Place well apart on a baking tin and bake for 10 minutes in a moderate oven (gas mark 4-5 or 375-400 degrees Fahr.). Be careful not to overcook—the biscuits should be barely coloured. Remove from tin and immediately sprinkle with caster sugar.

SHAH BISCUITS

> *3 oz. butter or margarine*
> *3 oz. Whitworth's soft brown sugar*
> *1 egg yolk*
> *1 tablespoon golden syrup*
> *6 oz. Whitworth's Self-raising Flour*
> *2 oz. rice or potato flour or cornflour*
> *Pinch of salt*
> *1 teaspoon ground ginger*
> *¼ teaspoon bicarbonate of soda*

Grease 3 baking sheets.

Cream the fat and sugar. Beat in the egg yolk and syrup until really light and creamy. In cold weather, it helps to warm the syrup a little. Add the sifted dry ingredients and work them in well. Roll walnut-sized pieces in the palms, flatten them a little and place on the baking sheets, allowing room for spreading. Bake in a fairly hot oven (gas mark 5-6 or 400-425 degrees Fahr.). until cracked, then finish off (15 minutes baking in all) at a lower temperature (gas mark 1-2 or 300 degrees Fahr.).

Note.—The above quantities make about 30 biscuits.

For a richer mixture, use only 5 oz. of Whitworth's Self-raising Flour.

SHREWSBURY BISCUITS

> *4 oz. butter or margarine*
> *4 oz. caster sugar*
> *1 egg yolk*
> *Grated rind of 1 lemon*
> *8 oz. Whitworth's Self-raising Flour*
> *Pinch of salt*

Cream the butter and sugar together until very creamy. Add the yolk of egg and beat well. Work in the lemon rind and the flour and salt, sifted together. Knead well. Roll out to less than ¼ in. thick and cut out into various shapes. Place on a greased baking sheet and bake for 15-20 minutes in a moderate oven (gas mark 3 or 350 degrees Fahr.).

SALT AND SUGAR

A pinch of salt in sweet things and a pinch of sugar in savoury ones bring out the flavour of both.

SCOTCH CRISPIES

3 oz. margarine
3 oz. caster sugar
2 tablespoons golden syrup or black treacle
3 oz. Whitworth's Self-raising Flour
¼ teaspoon salt
8 oz. breakfast oats

Melt together the margarine, sugar and syrup in a pan large enough to hold all the ingredients. Mix the flour, salt and oats. Add to the melted (not hot) ingredients and mix thoroughly. Press into a well-greased shallow tin (a Swiss Roll tin is excellent) and flatten to about ¼ in. thick. Bake for 30-35 minutes in a moderate oven (gas mark 4 or 375 degrees Fahr.). Take from oven and cut into small squares or fingers. When cold, remove from the tin.

WATER WAFERS

3 oz. Whitworth's Self-raising Flour
2 oz. cornflour or rice flour
¼ teaspoon salt
½ oz. melted lard
Water to mix

Sift the dry ingredients. Make a well in the centre and pour in the cooled fat and enough water to make a firm dough. Knead well and roll out as thinly as possible. Prick all over with a fork, cut into plain rounds and place on a greased baking sheet, bake for 15-20 minutes in a moderate oven (gas mark 3-4 or 350-375 degrees Fahr.).

HANOVER BISCUITS

4 oz. butter
3 oz. caster sugar
1 egg
½ lb. Whitworth's Self-raising Flour
Pinch of salt

Cream the butter and sugar. Add the egg yolk and half the white. Gradually mix in the flour, sifted with the salt. Roll out very thinly and cut into rounds. Bake for 10 minutes in a moderate oven (gas mark 4 or 375 degrees Fahr.). Sandwich each pair of biscuits with raspberry jam, while hot. When cold, ice with the following: add as much icing sugar to the remaining white of egg as it will take, then beat well.

FLAPJACKS (YORKSHIRE)

> 5 oz. margarine
> 2 oz. caster sugar
> 2 oz. black treacle
> 8 oz. breakfast oats
> ¼ teaspoon salt
> 1 oz. Whitworth's Self-raising Flour

Melt together the fat, sugar and treacle in a large saucepan. Mix the dry ingredients together and stir them into the barely warm mixture. Mix together. Press into a large Swiss Roll tin and bake for 30-40 minutes in a moderate oven (gas mark 3-4 or 350-375 degrees Fahr.). Cut into squares or fingers while still hot and place on a wire rack to become cold. Pack into airtight tins.

★ VANILLA WAFERS

> 4½ oz. butter or margarine
> 4½ oz. caster sugar
> 2 eggs
> 4½ oz. Whitworth's Self-raising Flour
> Pinch of salt
> ¼ teaspoon vanilla essence

Cream the fat and sugar very well and beat in the eggs, one at a time, with a little of the flour. Sift the flour and salt and add them with the essence.
Grease baking sheets or the inverted bottoms of baking tins. Drop teaspoonfuls of the mixture onto them and with the tip of the spoon spread them out with a swirl. Bake for 7 minutes in a hot oven (gas mark 7 or 450 degrees Fahr.).
Lift off and, if they have not dried out too much, you can place them over a rolling-pin so that they will curve like roof tiles. If they are too firm to bend, it is probably because the eggs were not large enough. In this case, add a little milk next time. With a little practice, you will make these wafers perfectly.

NUT WAFERS

As these little wafers are not in the oven long enough to brown the nuts, first brown 2-3 tablespoons chopped blanched almonds in the oven. After spreading the batter with the tip of the spoon, drop a few in the centre of each. They will be a beautiful brown in the centre of a yellow wafer with a brown border.
★ Basic Recipe

CATS' TONGUES

2 oz. (generous) butter
2 oz. caster sugar
2 medium-sized egg whites
2 oz. Whitworth's Self-raising Flour
A few drops vanilla essence

Well grease and flour baking sheets or inverted baking tins.
Warm a mixing basin by filling it with hot water. Empty and dry
thoroughly. Cut the butter into this and beat until very soft. Add the
sugar and beat again. Add the egg whites, a little at a time to avoid
curdling. Finally, lightly mix in the flour and essence.
Place in a piping-bag fitted with a ½-inch pipe. Pipe 2-2½-inch lengths
on to the tin, allowing for spreading. Let rest for 15 minutes, then bake
for 5-10 minutes on the top shelf of a fairly hot oven (gas mark 6-7 or
425-450 degrees Fahr.).

ALMOND TARTS (ROUND OR BOAT-SHAPED)

Flan Pastry (page 8)
Raspberry or apricot jam
2 oz. butter or margarine
2 oz. caster sugar
1 egg
2 oz. Whitworth's Self-raising Flour
Pinch of salt
1 oz. Whitworth's ground almonds
Almond essence to taste

Roll out the pastry to less than an eighth inch thick, if possible. Stamp
out fluted rounds and fit them into little round tins. Cut others into
ovals and fit them into small boat-shaped tins. Press well into the tins
and prick the bottoms. Place ½ teaspoonful seedless raspberry jam or
apricot jam in each.
To make the filling, mix the remaining ingredients as for a Victoria
Sponge Sandwich (page 36), adding the ground almonds with the flour.
Spread just enough on the jam to allow the filling to rise level with the
pastry. Bake for 20-25 minutes in a moderate oven (gas mark 4-5 or
375-400 degrees Fahr.).
When cold, spoon a very thin layer of glacé icing (page 84) on each tart
and, if liked, decorate with chopped browned almonds or walnuts.

ICINGS and ETCETERAS

GIVE THE CROWNING TOUCH
TO GOOD CAKES

Icing does for cakes what make-up does for ladies—makes beautiful cakes even more beautiful and helps along the less lucky ones. We have included an American recipe for boiled frosting which we think you will find invaluable.

★ AMERICAN OR BOILED FROSTING

4 tablespoons water
8 oz. granulated sugar
Vanilla or lemon essence
1 egg white

Put the water and sugar in a pan, leave for a little, then heat slowly until the sugar is dissolved. Boil without stirring until a little dropped from a spoon into cold water forms a ball (240-245 degrees Fahr.). Remove, cool a little, add the essence and gradually pour the syrup onto the stiffly beaten white of egg, beating all the time. Continue beating until thick enough to stay in place when spread on the cake.

★ *Basic Recipe*

Variation I: **Brown Sugar Frosting**
Use Whitworth's soft brown sugar in place of white and flavour with vanilla.

Variation II: **Caramel Frosting**
Use caramel flavour to taste, in place of vanilla.

Variation III: **Chocolate Frosting**
Break up 2 oz. bar chocolate, add to the syrup and beat into the egg white as quickly as possible.

Variation IV: **Marshmallow Frosting**
Cut up and add 6 marshmallow sweets to the syrup, then beat into the egg white.

ALMOND PASTE (OR ICING)

Here are the ingredients for icing the top of the 8-inch Christmas Cake on page 63. If both top and sides are to be iced, double the quantities.

> *8-10 oz. Whitworth's ground almonds*
>
> *4 oz. sieved icing sugar*
>
> *4 oz. caster sugar*
>
> *1 large egg*
>
> *¼ teaspoon almond essence*
>
> *¼ teaspoon vanilla essence*
>
> *Lemon juice as required*

Sift the ground almonds and sugars together into a basin. Beat the egg, essences and ½ teaspoon of lemon juice a little. Add to the first mixture and stir together with a wooden spoon. Turn on to a board and knead together to make a pliable paste which is moist enough but not too moist. If necessary, add more lemon juice. Knead until there are no joins visible.

Form into a ball and roll out to a round a trifle smaller than the top of the cake. Brush the top of the cake with apricot puree or seedless jam. Place the almond paste on it and gently roll it to reach the edge of the cake all round. Roll a straight-sided 2-lb. jam jar around the cake to make a nice even finish on top. Set aside to firm up and dry off a little.

Note. – To ice both top and sides, make double the amount of paste. Having brushed both top and sides with apricot puree or seedless jam, as above, divide the almond paste in two. Roll out one part into a strip long enough and deep enough to encircle the cake or, to make it easier to handle, cut it into two pieces. Trim the edges straight, then press the paste against the sides.

Roll out the other piece into a round slightly smaller than the top of the cake and place it in position. Gently pass the rolling pin over the top to make the paste reach the edges. Roll the straight-sided 2-lb. jam jar around the sides and gently pinch the joins together all round. Finish with another light rolling so that the top is level and the sides straight. A quicker and just as efficient a way is to roll out the whole piece of almond paste for the top and sides into a round to cover the top and reach from a third to halfway down the sides, then gently work down the paste to cover the whole of the sides. Roll the top level and the sides straight, as above.

ICING CAKES OF OTHER SIZES

For the almond paste for the top of a 6 to 6½-inch cake, use 7 oz. Whitworth's ground almonds, 3 oz. each of icing and caster sugar, 1 small egg, 3 drops vanilla essence, 2 to 3 drops almond essence and a few drops of lemon juice.
For both top and sides, double the amounts.
For the top of a 9-inch cake, use 13 to 14 oz. Whitworth's ground almonds, 5 oz. each of icing and caster sugar, 2 small eggs, ½ teaspoon vanilla essence, 3 to 4 drops almond essence and lemon juice as required.
Double the amounts for both top and sides.
For an 11-inch cake, use 1¼ lb. Whitworth's ground almonds, 8 oz. each of icing and caster sugar, 2 large eggs, ½ teaspoon vanilla essence, ¼ teaspoon almond essence and lemon juice as required.
This amount of paste should be enough for both top and sides of a Christmas Cake. For both top and sides of a Wedding Cake, however, double the amounts.

ROYAL ICING

The following quantities are for the coating of the tops and sides of an 8-inch Christmas or other cake. (For other sized cakes, see below.)

> *1 lb. sieved icing sugar*
> *2 egg whites*
> *1 teaspoon lemon juice*
> *1 scant dessertspoon glycerine (optional)*

Beat the egg whites just enough to blend together. Add the lemon juice, then gradually work in the sugar. Add the glycerine, if using it.

Work the icing together rather than beat it because beating introduces small bubbles which will spoil the finished icing. When it reaches the stage where it will not hold its shape for piping but is of a good consistency, spread it over the top and on the sides of the cake with a palette knife dipped in hot water, then smooth off the top by drawing a ruler or a long firm straight-bladed knife over the surface towards you. This will remove some of the icing but it will level it off. Return this excess icing to the bowl. Smooth the surface of the sides in the same way.

Keep the remaining icing covered with a damp cloth so that, if you wish to give the cake a second coat or finish with piping, it will not have formed a crust. If the cloth becomes dry, the icing will harden and will be of no use for piping or finishing the icing.

Note.—Two coats of Royal Icing may be applied to the cake, with an interval to allow the first to dry. If only one coat is used give the almond paste a thin coat of water icing (page 84) or slightly beaten white of egg and leave to dry thoroughly before applying the Royal Icing. This will act as a barrier between the almond paste and the Royal Icing and will prevent any stain from the cake or the almond paste leaking through and spoiling the finished appearance of the cake.

ROYAL ICING FOR OTHER CAKES

To coat a 6-6½-*inch cake,* use half the above quantities.
For a 9-*inch cake,* use half as much again of the listed ingredients.
To coat an 11-*inch cake,* double the quantities.

ROYAL ICING FOR PIPING (DECORATING)

Generally, for the piping, which should be applied when the foundation coating of Royal Icing is hard, make up about half the quantity required for covering the cake. Beat until it holds a sharp peak. Any left-over icing from the coating, provided it has been covered with a damp cloth, can also be beaten to the sharp peak stage and used for the decoration.

TO TINT ROYAL ICING

Experience has shown that the safest way to tint Royal Icing in pastel colours is to add 1-2 drops of culinary colouring to a teaspoon of the icing, then gradually work this or as much as is required into the remainder. In this way, a soft pale colour, not a too vivid one, can be achieved.

CHOCOLATE GLACÉ ICING

2 oz. plain bar chocolate
3 tablespoons water (approx.)
8 oz. icing sugar
½ teaspoon vanilla essence
1 teaspoon butter

Break the chocolate into small pieces. Place them with the water in a small pan and very slowly warm until melted. Do not allow to boil. Stir in the icing sugar, keeping the pan just warm enough for the hand to rest comfortably on it. Stir in the vanilla essence, then remove from the heat and stir in the butter.

To ice small cakes and eclairs: Have the icing in a soup plate over warm water to keep it from setting. Dip the tops of the cakes into it, drain off excess and leave to set. If any decorations are to be used, place them in position before the icing sets.

GLACÉ ICING (WATER ICING)

8 oz. sifted icing sugar
2-3 tablespoons warm water
Few drops of any flavouring essence
Culinary colouring as required

Gently stir the sugar and water together over a low heat. Do not let the pan become hotter than the hand can bear when placed on its bottom. Use the wooden spoon for this test: Gather some of the icing on the back of the spoon. If it coats it fairly well, it is ready. If too thin, add a little more sugar. If too thick, add a few drops of water. Add flavouring and colouring as required.

LEMON OR ORANGE GLACÉ ICING

Infuse very thin slivers of lemon or orange rind in lemon or orange juice to the amount required, or use half juice and half water. Strain into the sugar and proceed as above.

CHOCOLATE SAUCE (FOR PROFITEROLES)

2 oz. bar plain chocolate
3-4 tablespoons water

Break the chocolate into pieces and add to the water in a small pan. Warm very gently to melt the chocolate. Spoon it over the Profiteroles.

★ CHOCOLATE VELVET FUDGE ICING

1 teacup granulated sugar
1 oz. plain chocolate
Pinch of salt
¾ teacup warm water
Vanilla essence to taste

Boil the first four ingredients together. Do not stir. Test by dropping a little into cold water; if it forms a soft ball at once, it is ready. Remove carefully to the table, leave until the mixture is cool, then add the vanilla essence and beat to a spreading consistency. If you have cooked the fudge a little too long and it turns hard, add a teaspoon of hot water and beat again. That will bring it round.

Variation I: **Vanilla Velvet Fudge Icing**
Omit the chocolate and substitute milk for the water.

Variation II: **Nut Velvet Fudge Icing**
Add chopped walnuts or almonds to the first mixture half-way through the beating.

FEATHER ICING

This is one of the most effective finishes to an iced cake. Make enough Glacé Icing to coat the cake plus ¼ extra for decoration. Spread the white icing on the cake. Tint the remainder a warm pink or other suitable colour. Pipe it in thin lines ¾ to 1 in. apart on the still wet white icing. With the point of a skewer, draw lines the same distance apart all in one direction, crossing the piped lines at right angles. Then run the skewer in the opposite direction between these lines, drawing the piped lines out to give a "feathered" effect. Chocolate "feathers" on pale pink icing is very attractive.

FILLINGS for CAKES

APRICOT FILLING

2 tablespoons apricot puree or jam
1 tablespoon water
2 oz. margarine
4 oz. icing sugar

Warm the puree or jam and water together, then leave to cool.
Cream the margarine and sugar very well and gradually beat the apricot mixture into them—a little at a time, as it tends to separate.
Use to sandwich and ice sponge-cakes.

★ *Basic Recipe*

VANILLA PASTRY CREAM

This is a filling for spreading between Victoria Sponge Sandwich or any other layer cake.

> *2 egg yolks*
> *3 oz. caster sugar*
> *1½ oz. Whitworth's Plain Flour*
> *½ pint milk (scant)*
> *Vanilla essence*

Beat the egg yolks and sugar together. Gradually work in the flour. When well blended, slowly stir in the milk. Stir continuously over a low heat until the mixture barely comes to the boil, then simmer for a few minutes while the flour cooks. Do not boil. Remove and add vanilla essence to taste.

OTHER FLAVOURS: In place of vanilla, *almond* or *coffee* essence can be used. For *sherry* flavour, add at least a tablespoon of sherry. For *chocolate* flavour, work in 2 dessertspoons cocoa with the flour, or grate and add a 2-oz. bar of dessert chocolate.

★ BUTTER ICING (VANILLA, COFFEE or LEMON)

> *2 oz. butter*
> *4 oz. sifted icing sugar*
> *Vanilla, coffee or lemon essence*
> *A drop of culinary colouring, if desired*
> *A few drops of hot water*

Cream the butter and work in half the sugar. Add essence to taste, about a teaspoonful of hot water, and the remaining sugar. Beat until very creamy—the more you beat this the better it is.

Variation with **Chocolate**
Follow basic recipe, adding an extra ½ oz. butter. Work in a tablespoon cocoa or ½ oz. or so of melted chocolate with vanilla essence to taste and a teaspoon of left-over coffee.

French Variation
Follow basic recipe, using ½ oz. less butter and no water. Work in orange or lemon juice or sherry, brandy or rum in place of water.
★ *Basic Recipe*

86

TEA-TABLE SPECIALS

SCONES and QUICK BREADS

Even cake itself takes second place when there's a plate of hot scones on the tea-table— or some of the delicious fancy breads that can be made without yeast by using Whitworth's Self-raising Flour.

SUGGESTIONS FOR LIGHT SCONES

Always sift flour and salt together to aerate the mixture—that's one of the great secrets of lightness.

Mix, roll out and get ·your scones into the oven as quickly as possible. Too much handling makes for heaviness.

Scone dough hardly needs rolling—many good cooks simply *pat* it out. If you do use a rolling pin, use it *lightly*. With a scone cutter, cut straight down and lift up and out. A twist will make your scones lop-sided.

Make your scones not much more than half an inch deep; if they are thicker, the outside will bake too hard before the inside is cooked.

For piping-hot scones at short notice, keep a mixture of the rubbed-in ingredients on hand. This will keep for a week or more; and you can add liquid in a jiffy just before popping the scones into a hot oven.

To freshen stale scones, pass them quickly under the cold tap, then place them in a covered dish in a hot oven for a few minutes.

★ SCONES

8 oz. Whitworth's Self-raising Flour
¼-½ level teaspoon salt
1-1½ oz. margarine
¼ pint milk

Have a baking tin or sheet ready greased and floured. Sieve the flour and salt. Rub in the fat to fine breadcrumb stage and mix to a soft dough with the milk. Turn on to a floured board, shape lightly into one or two rounds and pat out to about ½ in. thick. Place on the prepared tin. Mark almost through in a cross and bake for 12-15 minutes in a hot oven (gas mark 7-8 or 450-475 degrees Fahr.). Or roll out ½-in. thick, cut into rounds and bake for 7-10 minutes.

Variation after Variation

SWEET SCONES

Add 1 tablespoon sugar to the dry ingredients.

FRUIT SCONES

Add 1-2 oz. Whitworth's sultanas or chopped dates to the sweet scone dough.

FADGE

Shape the plain scone or sweet scone dough into an oval bun and bake for 35-40 minutes in a moderately hot oven (gas mark 5 or 400 degrees Fahr.). Cut as for bread.

GRIDDLE (GIRDLE) SCONES

Follow the plain scone recipe and cut the dough into rounds ½ in. thick. Bake on both sides on a not-too-hot griddle (girdle), bakestone or frying-pan, for about 15 minutes in all.
★ *Basic Recipe*

SYRUP SCONES

Beat 1 tablespoon syrup into the milk in the plain scone recipe.

CHEESE SCONES

> *4 oz. Whitworth's Self-raising Flour*
> *Pinch of salt*
> *A few grains Cayenne pepper*
> *1 oz. butter or margarine*
> *1-1½ oz. grated dry cheese*
> *¼ pint (approx.) milk*

Mix together the flour, salt and Cayenne pepper. Rub in the fat. Add the cheese and enough milk to make a not-too-wet dough. Roll out, cut into rounds and bake as for plain scones.

DROP SCONES

> *8 oz. Whitworth's Self-raising Flour*
> *Pinch of salt*
> *1 tablespoon caster sugar*
> *1 walnut margarine*
> *1 egg*
> *1 teaspoon syrup*
> *1 teacup milk*
> *A few drops lemon essence*

Sift the flour, salt and sugar into a bowl. Rub in the fat. Beat together the egg and syrup, add the milk and stir into the dry ingredients. Add the essence. The batter should be like thick cream. Drop dessert spoonfuls on to the hot greased surface of a griddle (girdle), bakestone or frying-pan, and brown both sides, turning the scones just as bubbles begin to form.

STEAMED BREAD

> 2 teacups Whitworth's Self-raising Flour
> 1 teacup crushed Weetabix
> 1 teacup Whitworth's medium oatmeal
> ¼ teaspoon bicarbonate of soda
> ½ teaspoon salt
> 1 teacup Whitworth's sultanas
> 1 tablespoon Whitworth's soft brown sugar
> 1½ cups (approx.) thick sour milk
> 1 tablespoon black treacle

Have ready greased 3-4 straight-sided tins.

Mix the dry ingredients in a bowl. Stir in the sour milk and treacle, first beaten together. Turn into the prepared tins, put on the lids and steam for 2½-3 hours. Turn on to a wire rack to cool. Serve, cut into thin slices and buttered, for tea.

This bread is equally good with dates instead of sultanas or with the addition of chopped nuts.

Note.—Straight-sided or tube tins can easily be made by cutting the top off salt tins and hammering back the rough edges so that the loaf slips out without difficulty.

OVERNIGHT TEA LOAF

Don't be put off by the name. This is a simple recipe that is really delicious.

> 12 oz. Whitworth's Dried Fruit Mixture
> 4 oz. Whitworth's demerara sugar
> ¾ cup of strong cold tea
> 8 oz. Whitworth's Self-raising Flour
> 1 egg

Put the fruit and sugar in a bowl, pour over the cold tea and leave to stand overnight. Next day add the beaten egg and flour and mix well. Pour it into a greased and floured loaf tin and bake at gas mark 5 or 400 degrees Fahr., for about 1 hour.

Allow to cool. Cut into thin slices, and butter.

IRISH TREACLE BREAD

> 2 oz. butter or margarine
> ¼ pint (approx.) water
> 2 tablespoons black treacle
> 2 oz. Whitworth's soft brown sugar
> 1 egg
> 8 oz. Whitworth's Self-raising Flour
> ½ teaspoon ground ginger
> ½ teaspoon mixed spice
> Pinch of salt
> ¼ teaspoon bicarbonate of soda

Melt the fat in the water. Beat the treacle, sugar and egg together and add to the sifted dry ingredients. Add the cooled butter and water. (If the mixture is a little dry add more water.) Turn into a well-greased and floured loaf tin and bake for 1-1¼ hours in a moderate oven (gas mark 3-4 or 350-375 degrees Fahr.) until the loaf is firm to the touch.
Note.—To make a **Fruit Bread** add up to 4 oz. Whitworth's sultanas or seedless raisins.

WELSH LOAF

> 8 oz. Whitworth's Self-raising Flour
> 1 level teaspoon mixed spice
> Pinch of salt
> 3 oz. butter or margarine
> 3 oz. Whitworth's soft brown sugar
> 8 oz. Whitworth's Dried Fruit Mixture
> 1 oz. Whitworth's chopped candied peel
> 1 egg
> ¼ pint sour milk
> ¼ teaspoon bicarbonate of soda

Sift the dry ingredients together. Rub in the fat and then the sugar. Add the fruit (some of it cut in half) and the peel. Work in the beaten egg, then beat the sour milk and soda together and stir them into the mixture. Turn into a well-greased and floured loaf tin and bake for 1-1¼ hours in a moderate oven (gas mark 3-4 or 350-375 degrees Fahr.).

DATE SANDWICH

> ½ lb. chopped dates
> 1 teacup water
> Juice and grated rind of 1 lemon
> 1½ teacups Whitworth's Self-raising Flour
> 1¾ teacups breakfast oats
> ½ teaspoon salt
> 4 oz. margarine
> 1 teacup Whitworth's soft brown sugar

Stew the dates, water, lemon rind and juice to a thickish pulp.
Put the flour, rolled oats and salt into a bowl and rub in the fat. Stir in the sugar. Press half this mixture into a greased 8 inch cake tin. Spread the date pulp on it and cover with the remaining mixture. Press well down. Bake for 30-40 minutes in a moderate oven (gas mark 3-4 or 350-375 degrees Fahr.).

DATE-NUT LOAF

> 8 oz. Whitworth's Self-raising Flour
> ¼ teaspoon salt
> 2 oz. Whitworth's soft brown sugar
> 2 oz. butter or margarine
> 4 oz. chopped stoned dates
> 2 oz. chopped Whitworth's walnuts
> Milk to mix

Grease and flour a loaf tin.
Mix the sifted flour and salt with the sugar in a basin. Rub in the fat. Add the dates and walnuts and enough milk to make a mixture which falls easily from the spoon when it is lifted up and given a quick jerk.
Turn into the prepared tin and bake for 45-50 minutes in a moderate oven (gas mark 4-5 or 375-400 degrees Fahr.).

Note.—The flavour can be varied to make a quite a "different" loaf by sifting with the flour ¼ teaspoon grated nutmeg or ½ teaspoon mixed spice or ground ginger. The fruit can be varied too. Chopped stoned prunes, for instance, can be used in place of dates. In this case use an extra ounce of sugar to make up for the comparative tartness of the prunes.

BANANA BREAD

⅓ breakfastcup vegetable fat or margarine
⅔ cup caster sugar
2 well-beaten eggs
1¼ breakfastcups Whitworth's Self-raising Flour
½ teaspoon salt
¼ cup chopped Whitworth's walnuts
1 cup mashed bananas

Grease and flour a loaf tin.
Cream the fat and sugar very well. Add the beaten eggs, a little at a time, and beat well. Add the flour, sifted with the salt, and walnuts, alternately with the bananas and beat well.
Turn into the prepared tin and bake for ¾-1 hour in a moderate oven (gas mark 3-4 or 350-375 degrees Fahr.).
Or bake for 45 minutes in a 7-in. x 12-in. tin.
This bread is cut into slices and buttered.

DINNER ROLLS

8 oz. Whitworth's Self-raising Flour
½ teaspoon salt
2 oz. lard
¼ pint milk and water

Sift the flour and salt into a bowl and rub in the fat to the fine breadcrumb stage. Dot the surface with the liquid and stir together with a knife. Gather up, handling the dough as little as possible.
Cut into 7-8 pieces. Form into rounds or boat-shapes. Place on a greased baking-sheet and bake for 10-12 minutes in a hot oven (gas mark 7-8 or 450-475 degrees Fahr.).
For TEA SCONES, a teaspoonful of sugar may be added before the liquid.

MEASURING SYRUP OR HONEY

When measuring a spoonful or cupful of syrup, black treacle or honey, it is a good idea first to dip the spoon or cup in boiling water to heat it thoroughly, then dry it. The syrup, etc., will then "fall off" easily and quickly. If the syrup, etc., has to be added to liquid, put it in with the spoon itself, leave to dissolve, then remove the spoon.

93

"SINGIN' HINNIES"

Northumberland gave these "girdle" (griddle) cakes to the world. As they cook, they make a softly singing sound—hence the name. They *must* be eaten hot.

> *5-6 oz. lard*
> *8 oz. Whitworth's Self-raising Flour*
> *Pinch of salt*
> *½ teaspoon spice (optional)*
> *3 oz. Whitworth's currants*
> *1-1½ oz. caster sugar (optional)*
> *Milk to mix*

Before starting to make these little cakes, put the griddle on to heat through thoroughly, just as you would heat an omelet pan before mixing the eggs. Then rub the fat into the sifted flour and salt (and spice, if used). Add the currants and sugar. Work in enough milk to make a not-too-moist dough. Roll out ¼ in. thick and cut into rounds. Cook on both sides on the hot griddle, which you have rubbed very lightly with lard (12-15 minutes in all). Split, spread with butter and serve *hot* for tea.

IRISH POTATO CAKES

> *½ lb. Whitworth's Self-raising Flour*
> *1 teaspoon salt*
> *1 oz. butter or margarine*
> *½ lb. mashed potatoes*
> *¼ pint milk*

Sift the flour and salt and rub in the fat. Work this mixture into the potatoes and add the milk by degrees. Roll out to ¼ in. thick and cut into rounds. Bake both sides to a rich gold colour on a greased hot griddle (girdle), bakestone or frying-pan, using very little fat. Serve hot, with butter.

TEA ROLLS

> *1 lb. Whitworth's Self-raising Flour*
> *1 teaspoon salt*
> *Milk or milk and water*

Sift the flour and salt. Add enough liquid to make a stiff dough. Divide the mixture into about 16 pieces. Roll between the palms and bake on a greased and floured tin for 10 minutes in a hot oven (gas mark 7-8 or 450-475 degrees Fahr.).

94

AMERICAN STRAWBERRY SHORTCAKE

12 oz. Whitworth's Self-raising Flour
⅓ teaspoon salt
1½-2 oz. margarine or lard
1½-2 oz. caster sugar
About 1 teacup milk
1-1½ lb. ripe strawberries, sweetened to taste

Sift the flour and salt. Rub in the fat, as you would for scones. Add the sugar and enough milk to make a soft dough. Divide into two pieces and lightly knead into rounds. Roll out one to fit into a 6-7-in. tin. Brush with melted margarine. Roll out the other piece to fit on top. Bake for 15-20 minutes in a hot oven (gas mark 7-8 or 450-475 degrees Fahr.).

Take from the oven and split into two rounds. Spread with butter and sandwich with half the strawberries, crushed and sweetened to taste (It's a good idea to let the fruit stand for an hour or so with the sugar.) Cover with remaining crushed and sweetened berries. The dish really calls for whipped cream!

Note.—Strictly speaking, this is not a tea-time cake but a dinner sweet. It comes into this section, however, because it is made with the basic scone dough.

HONEY-SULTANA LOAF

3 oz. butter or margarine
3 oz. honey
1 egg
8 oz. Whitworth's Self-raising Flour
¼ teaspoon salt
2 oz. Whitworth's sultanas
Milk to mix

Well grease and flour a 1-lb. loaf tin.

Cream the fat until it is soft. Add the honey and beat very well together. Beat in the beaten egg. Sift the flour and salt and mix them in. Add the sultanas together with enough milk to make the mixture of a good dropping consistency. Turn into the prepared tin and bake for 45-50 minutes in a moderate oven (gas mark 3-4 or 350-375 degrees Fahr.). Or make into buns. Half fill greased and floured patty tins with the mixture and bake for 20 minutes in a moderately hot oven (gas mark 4-5 or 375-400 degrees Fahr.).

Note.—If honey is very thick and difficult to handle in cold weather, stand the jar or tin in warm water to thin it down. Use when almost cold.

95

SO MANY GOOD THINGS BEGIN WITH

BATTERS

Everyday favourites like Yorkshire Pudding or Toad-in-the-hole, special-occasion treats like Crepes Suzette or fruit fritters—they all have one thing in common: a smooth, well-beaten batter. The basic recipe is the same; for pancakes, the addition of a little melted butter or oil helps in cooking; and, for fritters, the batter must be thicker, so that it will coat the food to be fried.

NOTES FOR NOVICES

Do let your batter stand for an hour or two before cooking.

Do have the fat smoking hot before pouring in a Yorkshire Pudding batter. Heat the tin with the fat in it in the oven for a few minutes first.

Don't let fritters delay on the way to table—they should be eaten as soon as possible. But you can make pancakes well beforehand and heat them up with a sizzling sauce, sweet or savoury.

★ YORKSHIRE PUDDING

> *4 oz. Whitworth's Plain Flour*
> *¼ teaspoon salt*
> *1-2 eggs*
> *¼ pint milk*
> *¼ pint lukewarm water*
> *1-2 oz. dripping*

Sift the flour and salt into a bowl. Make a well in the centre and drop in the whole egg or eggs. Gradually work the liquid into the mixture with a fork or whisk and beat well.

To bake a Yorkshire Pudding

Melt the fat in a roasting tin and make it very hot. Pour in the batter and bake for 25-30 minutes in a hot oven (gas mark 7-8 or 450-475 degrees Fahr.).

Savoury Variation

To make Yorkshire Pudding especially tasty, chop 1-2 medium-sized onions, immerse them in boiling water, drain and add to the above batter together with ½ teaspoon mixed herbs, if liked. Bake as above.

Add fruit for a simple sweet

Any sweetened stewed fruit—rhubard or dried apricots, for instance—is nice for this. Make the basic Yorkshire Pudding and, as soon as it comes from the oven and settles a little, pour on the hot fruit and serve at once.

SAUSAGE TOAD

> *Yorkshire Pudding batter, as above*
> *¾ lb. sausage meat*

Form the sausage meat into small balls. Place in a dripping tin and bake for 5 minutes in a hot oven (gas mark 7 or 450 degrees Fahr.). There should then be enough fat. If not, add a little extra. Pour the batter into the hot fat over the sausage balls and bake for 30 minutes at the above temperature. Serves four.

Variation—with Chops

Instead of sausage meat, use mutton or lamb chops. Prick the fatty places to encourage the fat to flow. Bake in the oven for 10 minutes, then add the batter and bake as above.

Variation—with Corned Beef

Mix chopped corned beef with the batter, pour into hot fat and bake as above.

★ *Basic Recipe*

★ PANCAKES

Add a dessertspoon melted butter or olive oil to basic Yorkshire Pudding batter. Use lard for frying. The addition of melted butter or olive oil to the basic batter not only gives a more delicate texture to pancakes but also enables you to make them paper thin without any fear of their sticking to the pan. Stir this into the batter just before cooking. Use *two* frying pans for best results; preferably the 6 or 7 inch size. Put them to warm over a low heat and, just before pouring in the batter, melt a small hazel nut of lard in each pan. Put not quite 2 tablespoons of batter into each pan and swirl it around to coat the bottom. Toss or turn with a palette knife when the underside is a pale gold and brown lightly on the second side. Have ready on the table a piece of greaseproof paper sprinkled with caster sugar. Drop each pancake on it, add a squeeze of lemon juice and roll up.

Variations with a Ritzy flavour

CREPES SUZETTE

Make 8 or 10 pancakes from the basic batter and have them ready, unrolled. Rub several lumps of sugar very hard on the rind of a ripe orange to absorb the essence. Put them in a large frying pan with ¼ pint orange juice and, if you can spare it, a tablespoon Curacao. Add 2 walnuts butter. Heat this sauce and place the pancakes in it, one at a time. As each becomes heated through, fold it in four and slip to one end of the pan to keep hot.
Serve with remaining sauce poured over the pancakes.

CREPES FLAMBES

Once you have made and folded the Crepes Suzette, sprinkle them with sugar when they are still in the pan, then pour over them a wine-glass of Curacao or Grand Marnier or brandy, first warmed a little. Set alight and serve when the flames die down.

APPLE PANCAKE ROLLS

Make the pancakes as in the basic recipe. Have ready hot apple sauce (made with whole Bramley Seedlings and a little cider) sieved and sweetened to taste. Spread a portion on each hot pancake, roll up and serve with a sprinkling of icing sugar and ground cinnamon well mixed.
★ *Basic Recipe*

PANCAKES WITH VANILLA CUSTARD

Make the pancakes as in the basic recipe (page 98). Prepare your favourite vanilla custard, twice as thick as usual, enriching it with evaporated milk. Spread thickly on the pancakes and roll up.

PANCAKES WITH BANANA FILLING

Make the pancakes as in the basic recipe. Mash 1-2 ripe bananas with a little lemon juice. Blend into thick hot vanilla custard, heat through, spread on the pancakes and roll up. Crushed pineapple, drained, makes another delicious filling.

Main Dish Variations—Very Tasty

PANCAKES WITH CREAMED CHICKEN

Make 8-10 pancakes as in the basic recipe. Spread with minced left-over chicken mixed with a rich white sauce. Roll up and place side by side in an oven-dish. Pour a little more white sauce over them, sprinkle with grated cheese and brown a little under the grill.

PANCAKES WITH CREAMED FISH

Make the pancakes as in the basic recipe. Make a filling as above but using flaked cooked fish and saving a little white sauce to spread over the rolled pancakes. Spread the pancakes with the filling and proceed as above. Cooked smoked haddock is excellent.

PANCAKES WITH CURRY FILLING

Make 8-10 pancakes as in the basic recipe. Melt 1 oz. fat. Add a chopped small onion and fry it to a pale gold. Blend in 1 tablespoon flour and 1 heaped teaspoon curry-powder and cook together for a minute. Blend in ¾ pint stock and seasoning to taste; simmer while stirring. Add a little chutney and a teaspoon of red currant jelly, if available, and simmer to the desired consistency. Work through a sieve. To half the sauce, add a teacup chopped meat or chicken or flaked cooked fish. Spread the mixture on the pancakes and roll up. Place in a shallow oven dish, pour the remaining curry sauce over (diluted, if necessary), heat through in the oven and serve.

FRITTERS

FRITTERS *call for a thicker batter*

Use the basic Yorkshire Pudding recipe but with only *half* the given quantity of liquid. Add 1 dessertspoon salad oil. Mix fritter batter very little as over-beaten batter "pulls off" what it coats.

APPLE FRITTERS

Cut peeled and cored apples into thin rings. Dip in flour, then in the batter and fry a golden brown in hot fat. Sprinkle with icing or caster sugar and serve at once.

BANANA FRITTERS

Slice bananas at an angle, dip in flour and proceed as above.

DATE FRITTERS

Make the basic batter as for Yorkshire Pudding, using only ¼ pint lukewarm water and reserving the egg white. Chop 4 oz. stoned dates and add to batter. Let stand for half an hour and fold in the stiffly beaten egg white. Drop spoonfuls into hot fat and fry to a golden brown. Sprinkle with caster sugar.

FISH IN BATTER

Put a tablespoon seasoned flour into a paper bag and drop the pieces of fish into it. Shake well to coat with the flour. Dip the fish into the batter and let any excess drain off. Drop into almost smoking-hot fat and fry until cooked through. Fillets of plaice and sole will be cooked in a matter of 3-4 minutes, so watch them and do not keep the fat at too high a temperature. For thicker pieces of fish like cod, hake or haddock fillets, have the fat very hot but, once the coating has become a pale gold, lower the temperature a little so that the inside of the fish will cook through.

WAFFLES

> *8 oz. Whitworth's Self-raising Flour*
> *Pinch of salt*
> *2 eggs*
> *2-3 tablespoons melted butter*
> *¼ pint milk*

These American favourites are well-liked in this country, but you must have a waffle iron to make them successfully. For the batter, sift flour and salt into a bowl. Drop in the egg yolks and cooled melted butter, then gradually beat in ¼ pint milk. Fold in the stiffly beaten whites. If the mixture is not thin enough to pour easily, add a little more milk. Heat the waffle iron and grease it lightly with lard or vegetable oil. Place a tablespoon batter in the centre so that it will spread out without oozing between the top and bottom irons. Put down the heated top and wait until the steam no longer comes from between the irons. Then, using the points of a two-pronged fork, remove the waffles, beautifully crisp and clean. Serve with slightly thinned golden syrup or, if you can get it, maple syrup.

SAVOURY VARIATIONS FOR SNACKS

Use the waffles as the foundation for any tasty morsels—fried bacon and egg, sausages and tomato, creamed mushrooms or creamed fish. Place these on top of a golden-brown waffle and serve very hot.

CHEESE POP-OVERS

Make the batter as for Yorkshire Pudding, adding 3 tablespoons grated sharp dry cheese and 1 dessertspoon melted margarine at the last minute. Put a small nut of fat into each of 9 small patty tins and place them in the oven to get hot (gas mark 7 or 450 degrees Fahr.). Pour in the batter, one third full, and bake until crisp and golden. These are a treat for tea. Without the cheese, they are a delicious accompaniment to any meal.

FRITTER BATTERS

Fritter Batters are better if left to rest for an hour or so before being used, because the elasticity introduced by beating is relaxed. Batter which is well beaten and then used immediately will not adhere to whatever it is to coat. The elasticity pulls whatever it covers away from it. If batter must be used at once, mix it very gently with no beating whatever.

101

INSPIRATIONS FOR

PUDDINGS

To children, the most important part of a meal, usually, is the pudding. And men are like children in this way—oftener than is supposed. So it's well worth a woman's while to specialise in this delicious department of cooking.

Leaving out milk puddings (you will have you own favourites amongst these), there are only three main types—sponge puddings, suet puddings and baked puddings, usually made with fresh or bottled fruit. Master the method for each of these and you can vary them in countless ways to suit the season and your own family's preferences.

APPLE AMBER

> *4 oz. short crust pastry (page 8)*
> *1 lb. cooking apples*
> *1 tablespoon water*
> *1-1½ oz. butter or margarine*
> *3-4 oz. caster sugar*
> *2 eggs*

Line a glass pie-dish with the rolled-out pastry.
Wash the apples, slice them and stew them in the water until tender.

Rub through a sieve. Beat the butter, 2½ oz. sugar and egg yolks together, then stir them into the sieved apples. Turn into the pastry-lined dish and bake for about 25-30 minutes in a moderately hot oven (gas mark 5-6 or 400-425 degrees Fahr.) until the pastry is browned.
Whip the egg whites very stiffly. Sprinkle with half the remaining sugar and again whip until the mixture holds a peak. Sprinkle the remaining sugar on top and fold it in. Pile on top of the apples, making sure that it covers the pastry. If you want a nice crisp surface, sprinkle with a further teaspoon of sugar. Bake for a further 30 minutes in a coolish oven (gas mark 2-3 or 325-350 degrees Fahr.).
Very good, hot or cold.

★ VANILLA SOUFFLE

> *1 oz. butter*
> *1 oz. Whitworth's Self-raising or Plain Flour*
> *¼ pint milk*
> *3 egg yolks*
> *½ oz. caster sugar*
> *½ teaspoon vanilla essence*
> *4 egg whites*

Well grease the soufflé dish which can be white china or oven glass. It is a ribbed dish in order to get a quick entry of heat and also a larger distribution of heat. Amounts are for a 6½-in. soufflé dish.
Melt the butter in a saucepan, add the flour, gently cook without browning for 1 minute. Remove and stir in the milk so that the mixture will be smooth. Return to the heat, stir and cook gently until the mixture will leave the sides of the pan. Remove and drop in the yolks, one at a time. Beat thoroughly. Stir well so that all the mixture is well blended. Sprinkle the sugar over the top and add the vanilla essence.
Whip the egg whites until they are stiff and dryish. Drop into the other mixture and, with a metal spoon, fold them over and over, passing the spoon around the inside of the bowl to bring the sides into the mixture. This is known as the "soufflé cut". Do not stir.
Turn into the prepared soufflé dish. There should be enough of the mixture only to half fill the dish. With the tip of a teaspoon, make a line ¼ in. deep ¾ in. inside the rim all round. Place in the upper half of a moderately hot oven, not too near the top, and bake for 20-25 minutes (gas mark 5-6 or 400-425 degrees Fahr.). If you like the soufflé very soft, 20 minutes will be enough. If you want it firmer, give it 25 or even 30 minutes, but the softer the better. It should, of course be pale gold on top.
★ *Basic Recipe*

ORANGE SOUFFLE

Follow the above recipe, omitting the vanilla essence and adding the grated rind of 1-2 oranges.

CHOCOLATE SOUFFLE

Melt a 2-oz. bar of plain chocolate in 1 tablespoon water over a low heat. When smooth, stir into the white sauce, then proceed as for Vanilla Soufflé.

PINEAPPLE SOUFFLE

Place 1-2 tablespoons of drained crushed pineapple in the soufflé dish, then add the Vanilla Soufflé mixture and bake as above.

APPLE SPONGE PUDDING

1½-2 lb. apples
Sugar to taste
1-2 tablespoons water
Grated lemon rind
1-2 cloves
6 oz. Whitworth's Self-raising Flour
Pinch of salt
2 oz. butter or margarine
2 oz. caster sugar
1 egg
¼ pint milk
(Enough for 4 or 5 helpings)

Peel, core and slice the apples and stew them with sugar to taste, water, lemon rind and cloves. Leave until cold. Rub fat into sifted flour and salt. Beat sugar and egg together, add milk and stir the mixture into the rubbed ingredients. Turn the apples into a greased pudding dish, add the batter and bake for 40-50 minutes in a moderately hot oven (gas mark 5 or 400 degrees Fahr.).

This pudding is the "father and mother" of any number of others. By adding the larger quantities of flour and milk, you will get a bigger but slightly less rich pudding.

> *4 oz. butter*
> *4 oz. caster sugar*
> *2 eggs*
> *4-6 oz. Whitworth's Self-raising Flour*
> *¼ teaspoon salt*
> *2-3 tablespoons milk*
> *A few drops vanilla essence*
> (Enough for 4 to 6 helpings)

Cream the butter and sugar very well. Beat in the eggs, one at a time, adding a pinch or so of the flour if the mixture looks like separating and continue beating. Add the sifted flour and salt, milk and vanilla essence. Do not over-beat the pudding if you want it really light and delicious. Two-thirds fill a well-greased pudding basin with the mixture. Cover with a double thickness of greased greaseproof paper and secure this safely. Stand in boiling water coming at least a third way up the basin. Cover and steam for 1½ hours. Serve with Jam Sauce (page 107 under Castle Puddings).

Variations—Very Good

FRUIT SPONGE

To the above Canary Sponge Pudding recipe, add 6 oz. Whitworth's Dried Fruit Mixture, then follow the directions.

CHERRY SPONGE

Cut up 2 to 3 oz. Whitworth's Glacé Cherries. Add them to the Canary Sponge Pudding Mixture, then follow the recipe.

CHOCOLATE SPONGE

Allow an extra tablespoon milk. Dissolve 1-1½ oz. bar chocolate in the milk, warming it just enough to do so. Beat in alternately with the flour. Serve with custard sauce.

★ *Basic Recipe*

105

COFFEE SPONGE

Add a tablespoon coffee essence and ½ teaspoon vanilla essence, reducing the amount of milk accordingly. Serve with vanilla-flavoured custard sauce.

ESSEX SPONGE

Spread any favourite jam thickly all over the inside of the greased basin. Add the sponge mixture and steam for 1½ hours.

GINGER SPONGE

Sift 1 teaspoon ground ginger with the flour and salt. Serve with ginger-flavoured custard sauce.

JAM CAP SPONGE

Place 2-4 tablespoons jam or marmalade in the bottom of the well greased basin before adding the sponge mixture. When turned out, the jam will spread all over the pudding.

LEMON OR ORANGE SPONGE

Add the grated rind of a lemon or orange to the creamed mixture. Serve with clear lemon or orange sauce.

RASPBERRY SPONGE

Reduce the sugar by 2 oz. Mix in 2-3 oz. raspberry jam with the flour. Serve with custard or Jam Sauce.

CASTLE PUDDINGS

1½ oz. butter or margarine
1½ oz. caster sugar
1 egg
3 oz. Whitworth's Self-raising Flour
Pinch of salt
A little milk
Hot jam sauce
(Enough for 4 individual puddings)

Cream the fat and sugar. Beat in the egg. Fold in the sifted flour and salt with enough milk to make a soft batter. Half fill greased and floured dariole moulds, cover with greaseproof paper and steam for 50 minutes. Turn out and serve with hot jam sauce. To make this, bring to the boil 3 tablespoons jam. 3 tablespoons water and 1 dessertspoon lemon juice.

★ SUET PUDDING

I	*II*
4 oz. Whitworth's Self-	*6 oz. Whitworth's Self-*
raising Flour	*raising Flour*
2 oz. fine breadcrumbs	*Pinch of salt*
Pinch of salt	*2-3 oz. finely chopped suet*
2-3 oz. finely chopped suet	*Cold water to mix*
Cold water to mix	

(Enough for 4 or 5 helpings)

Follow either of the above recipes. Mix the dry ingredients. Add the suet and enough water to make a softish dough. Turn into a greased pudding basin, two-thirds filling it. Cover with greased greaseproof paper. Stand in boiling water, cover and steam for 1½ hours. Turn out and serve with hot jam or golden syrup.

Variations again

SPOTTED DOG

Add 3-4 oz. Whitworth's Dried Fruit Mixture and a little chopped candied peel to Recipe I.

★ *Basic Recipe*

APPLE PUDDING

Follow Basic Recipe II. Line a greased pudding basin with two-thirds of the pastry. Fill with sliced apples (or rhubarb cut in 1 in. pieces, or plums or other fresh fruit). Add sugar to taste but see that it does not come in contact with the pastry. Add up to a tablespoon cold water. Damp the edges of the pastry. Roll out remaining piece, place on top and pinch edges together. Cover with greaseproof paper and steam or boil for 2-2½ hours. Turn out on to a deepish dish in case the pudding breaks.

ROLY-POLY

Follow Basic Suet Recipe II (page 107). Roll out in a rectangular piece ¼ in. thick. Spread with jam or marmalade, leaving a margin all round. Moisten the edges and roll up. Press the ends to seal them and dust with flour. Wrap in a cloth, first scalded and dusted with flour, leaving it a little loose around the pudding but securing the ends tightly. Place in boiling water and boil for 1½-2 hours. Unwrap and sprinkle with sugar. Serve with vanilla custard sauce.

Note.—Suet Pastry No. II—that is, without breadcrumbs—is the better one to use for any pudding which has to be immersed in water.

JAM ROLL, BAKED

Use Suet Pastry I (page 107) or Short Crust (page 8). Roll out as for Roly-Poly (above) and spread with jam, leaving a margin. Brush this with water, roll up and place in a greased tin. Brush with milk and bake for 40 to 45 minutes in a moderately hot oven (gas mark 5 or 400 degrees Fahr.). When the baked Roll comes from the oven, sprinkle with caster sugar.

LAYERED SYRUP PUDDING

Use Basic Recipe I or II (page 107). Divide the pastry into 4 pieces, from small to one large enough to line the basin. Line the basin and put 1-2 tablespoons golden syrup and a teaspoon or so of lemon juice into it. Sprinkle in a tablespoon breadcrumbs or crushed Weetabix. Cover with a piece of pastry rolled out to fit. Put in a second layer of syrup, lemon juice and crumbs and cover with another piece of rolled-out pastry. Repeat, finish with suet pastry. Cover with greased paper and steam for 2-2½ hours.

LAYERED JAM PUDDING

Follow preceding recipe, using jam instead of syrup.

LEMON SUET PUDDING

Use either No. I or II Basic Recipe (page 107). Line a greased bowl with two-thirds of the pastry. Deeply prick a whole lemon all over and place in in the centre of the bowl. Add 4-5 oz. brown sugar. Wet the edges of the pastry. Roll out the remaining piece, place it on top and pinch together. Cover as above and steam for 1½-2 hours. Turn out and serve with its own lemon syrup. The family will probably insist on having the lemon, too.

Note.—Golden syrup may be used in place of brown sugar.

CHRISTMAS PUDDING—*Make it in November!*

3 oz. Whitworth's Self-raising Flour
½ teaspoon grated nutmeg
½ teaspoon ground cinnamon
1 shallow teaspoon mixed spice
½ teaspoon salt
4 oz shredded suet
4 oz. breadcrumbs
4 oz. sugar (Whitworth's Demerara, for preference)
24 oz. Whitworth's Dried Fruit Mixture
Grated rind of 1 small lemon
2 eggs
Cider, old ale or milk to mix (about 1 teacup)
(Enough for 1 large pudding or 2 small ones)

Sift the flour, spices and salt together. Stir in the suet, crumbs, sugar, fruit and lemon rind. Beat the eggs and stir them into the mixture together with enough liquid to give a soft dropping consistency.

Turn into a well greased pudding basin, 2½ pint size, and cover with greased greaseproof paper, and a clean pudding cloth, securely tied. Stand in boiling water coming half-way up the basin, cover with a tight fitting lid, and boil for 6 hours (or 4 hours in 2 basins).

Remove, allow to cool, and take off the cloth, but leave the greaseproof paper without disturbing it. Cover with another piece of fresh greaseproof paper on top of the old, and a clean cloth. Store in a cool, dry place. Boil for 3 hours before serving.

Note.—Do use a basin which is free from cracks and reasonably new, otherwise there is a danger of the pudding not keeping.

CARROT PUDDING

This pudding can quite well be served as an inexpensive Christmas
Pudding. Make on Christmas Day.

> *3 oz. Whitworth's Self-raising Flour*
> *3 oz. breadcrumbs*
> *2 oz. Whitworth's Demerara sugar*
> *¼ teaspoon salt*
> *1 teaspoon mixed spice*
> *3-4 oz. chopped suet*
> *½ lb. Whitworth's Dried Fruit Mixture*
> *½ breakfastcup grated raw potatoes*
> *1 tablespoon black treacle*
> *½ breakfastcup grated raw carrots*
> *Pinch of bicarbonate of soda*
> *A little orange or lemon juice to mix*
> (Enough for 6 helpings)

Grease a 2½-pint pudding basin.
Mix the ingredients in the order given, adding just enough liquid to
make a fairly easy dropping batter. Turn into the basin, cover with
greased paper and steam for 2½-3 hours. Serve with any sweet or
custard sauce.

Putting the Apples into
APPLE DUMPLINGS

> *½ lb. short crust pastry (page 8)*
> *4 cooking apples*
> *4 dessertspoons Whitworth's Demerara sugar*
> (For 4 dumplings)

Divide the pastry into four, form into balls and roll out. Peel and core
the apples. Place each on a round of pastry and fill the centres with
sugar. Put a tiny nut of margarine into each cavity. Wet the edges of the
pastry and pinch them together to encase the apples.
To bake, place, joined side down, on a greased tin and brush with milk
or sugar syrup. Bake in a hot oven (gas mark 5-6 or 400-425 degrees
Fahr.) for 30-45 minutes, depending on the size of the apples. If fairly
large, better lower the heat after 20 minutes.
To boil, tie each dumpling separately in a floured pudding cloth wrung
out in hot water. Drop into boiling water and boil gently for 50
minutes.
Use half sugar and half sultanas to fill the centres or put a clove or a
pinch of ground cinnamon with the sugar.

UPSIDE-DOWN PUDDING

2 tablespoons Whitworth's soft brown sugar
1 tablespoon butter or margarine
Pineapple rings (tinned) or stoned dates, any fruit
4 oz. butter or margarine
4 oz. caster sugar
2 eggs
Pinch of salt
6 oz. Whitworth's Self-raising Flour
Lukewarm milk
(Enough for 5 or 6 helpings)

Cream the brown sugar and fat together and line the inside of a deep oven dish with them. Decorate the bottom and lower sides of the dish with the pineapple or dates. Cream the other fat and sugar and beat in the beaten eggs and salt. Fold in the flour and add just enough lukewarm milk to make not too soft a mixture. Pour into the prepared dish and bake for 45 minutes in a moderate oven (gas mark 3 or 350 degrees Fahr.). Turn out and serve with thin custard sauce or, if pineapple is selected, the juice from a large tin, thickened with a little arrowroot.

★ OVEN PANCAKES

2 oz. Whitworth's Self-raising Flour
Pinch of Salt
2 oz. butter
2 oz. caster sugar
2 eggs
3/8 pint of milk

Sift the flour and salt. Cream the fat and sugar very well, then beat in the eggs, one at a time. Add a little flour and a little milk alternately until all is used up. Mix well. Half fill well greased saucers with the batter and bake for 12-15 minutes in a moderately hot oven (gas mark 4-5 or 375-400 degrees Fahr.). Turn on to a paper sprinkled with sugar and serve with sugar and lemon or hot jam sauce (page 107, under Castle Puddings).

Variation I:
Add up to a dozen currants to each portion of batter before baking in the oven.

Variation II:
Instead of currants, add 1-2 chopped walnuts and a little chopped crystallised ginger in the same way.

★ *Basic Recipe.*

111

PLUM CRUMB PUDDING

> 1½ lb. plums
> A little water
> 1-2 tablespoons golden syrup
> 6 oz. Whitworth's Self-raising Flour
> ¼ teaspoon salt
> 2½ oz. margarine
> 2 oz. caster sugar
> (Enough for 4 to 6 helpings)

Place the plums, water and syrup in a greased shallow oven dish and bake to soften the fruit. Leave to cool. Sift the flour and salt together and rub the fat into them. Stir in the sugar. Sprinkle the "crumbs" over the plums and bake for 25-30 minutes in a moderately hot oven (gas mark 4-5 or 375-400 degrees Fahr.).
Any fruit can be used this way. Rhubarb is particularly good.

DUTCH APPLE CAKE

> 4 oz. Whitworth's Self-raising Flour
> ¼ teaspoon salt
> 1 oz. caster sugar
> 1 oz. butter or margarine
> ½ teaspoon vanilla essence
> Milk or water to mix
> ¾ lb. apples
> 1-2 oz. caster sugar
> 1 teaspoon ground cinnamon
> Juice and grated rind of 1 lemon
> 2-3 oz. butter or margarine
> (Enough for 6 helpings)

Sift the flour and salt. Stir in the 1 oz. sugar and chop in the fat until like coarse oatmeal. Add the essence and milk or water to make a soft dough. Roll out to fit a greased tin, 8 in. square.
Cut the peeled and cored apples into thin wedges and press them, sharp side down, into the dough. Sprinkle with the other sugar and spice, mixed together, then with the lemon juice and grated rind. Pour melted fat over the top and bake for 35-45 minutes in a moderately hot oven (gas mark 4-5 or 375-400 degrees Fahr.).

CHOCOLATE PUDDING (EGGLESS)

10 tablespoons hot water
1 rounded tablespoon black treacle
3 oz. margarine or lard
8 oz. Whitworth's Self-raising Flour
¼ teaspoon salt
3 oz. caster sugar
1 oz. cocoa or chocolate powder
½ teaspoon vanilla essence
¼ teaspoon coffee essence
¼ teaspoon bicarbonate of soda

Grease a two-pint pudding basin.

Measure the water into a jug. Add the black treacle with the spoon itself and leave to dissolve, then remove the spoon. Melt the fat and leave it to cool.

Sift the flour, salt, sugar and cocoa or chocolate powder into a largish bowl. Add the essences and soda to cooled treacle water and stir into the dry ingredients. Stir in the cooled but still liquid fat.

Turn into the prepared basin and cover with greaseproof paper. Stand the basin on a trivet with boiling water coming half-way up. Cover and steam for 1½ hours. Serve a vanilla-flavoured custard sauce with this pudding.

APPLE CHARLOTTE

1½ to 2 lb. apples
4 oz. Whitworth's Demerara or Soft Brown Sugar
Grated lemon peel
A few Whitworth's washed sultanas
Slices of bread and butter

Grease a pie dish, line it with slices of bread and butter, butter side inwards. Peel, core and slice the apples, and pack them in the dish in layers, interspersed with the sugar, and a sprinkling of sultanas or other fruit to taste. A layer of bread and butter may also be included, and the top should finally be covered with a layer of bread and butter and a final sprinkling of sugar. Bake in a moderately hot oven (gas mark 5 or 400 degrees Fahr.) for three-quarters to one hour, or until nicely browned.

113

'DIFFERENT' IDEAS

FROM FAR-AWAY PLACES

In this section, we have gathered together a group of unusual recipes which are unusually good. Some come from the Continent, some from America—all are within the range of the average home cook. Do try them!

AMERICAN DOUGHNUTS

>*2 teacups Whitworth's Self-raising Flour*
>*Pinch of salt*
>*Pinch of grated nutmeg*
>*¼ teaspoon ground cinnamon*
>*1 tablespoon margarine or butter*
>*½ teacup caster sugar*
>*1 egg*
>*Milk to form a fairly stiff dough*

Sift the first four ingredients. Cream the fat and sugar until light. Beat in the egg, then add the dry ingredients and milk alternately.

Sprinkle the pastry board with a little flour and lightly roll out the dough to ½ inch thick. Cut out rounds with a 2-2½-inch plain cutter, then cut out the centres with a ¾-inch cutter. Leave to rest on the board, uncovered, for 20-25 minutes, while the deep fat or oil is getting hot. When a tiny cube of bread, dropped in, becomes a pale gold in 60 seconds, the fat is ready for the doughnuts. (If you use a thermometer, the temperature should be 360-365 degrees Fahr.).

Fry a few at a time, so the fat doesn't cool and make the doughnuts greasy. Fry for 3-5 minutes in all, turning the doughnuts as they rise. Drain on absorbent paper, sprinkle with icing or caster sugar and serve either hot or cold.

Make doughnut balls of the cut-out centres and fry them in the same way.

114

APFEL STRUDEL (VIENNESE)

Strudel pastry is to the Austrian what puff pastry is to the French and short pastry is to the British housewife. It is best known in Apfel (Apple) Strudel, but the paste can be used for quite a number of sweet and savoury dishes in the same way that puff pastry and short crust pastry are used in many ways.

Paste:

8 oz. Whitworth's Self-raising Flour
Pinch of salt
1 egg
1 tablespoon salad oil
Water

Filling:

2-3 walnuts butter
2 tablespoons breadcrumbs
1 tablespoon chopped Whitworth's almonds
1 lb thinly sliced good cooking apples
3 tablespoons Whitworth's currants and sultanas, mixed
2-3 oz. Whitworth's Demerara sugar
Lemon juice

Sift the flour and salt on to a pastry-board. Make a well in the centre. Add the egg and oil, with enough water to make about ¼ pint. Be sparing with the water, remember. Work together to a pliable dough. When it no longer sticks to the hands, leave it for an hour on the board, with a large warm bowl over it. To keep the bowl warm, place a cloth in hot water, wring out as dry as possible and spread it over the bowl.

Place a large clean cloth on the table and sprinkle a very little flour over it. Place the paste in the centre and begin to roll out, then pull and stretch the dough until it is paper thin. This is a job which calls for skill and care to avoid making any holes in the paste. When it is very thin and almost transparent, brush the surface with a little of the melted butter. Put half the remainder of the butter into a small bowl and fry the crumbs in the rest.

Sprinkle the fried crumbs over the pastry. Then spread the almonds, apples, dried fruit and sugar on top. Sprinkle with lemon juice and roll up as you would a Swiss Roll. Place in a semi-circle on a large greased baking-tin. Brush with the remaining melted butter and bake for 40-45 minutes, starting in a hot oven (gas mark 7-8 or 450-475 degrees Fahr.) then, when the colour is pale gold, lower the heat to gas mark 4 or 375 degrees Fahr. Finish off with a little caster sugar, place on a hot platter and cut into thickish rounds.

FRENCH FRUIT TART

> ¼ lb. puff pastry (page 7)
> Fresh fruit
> Icing sugar

Roll out the pastry in a strip or square ¼ in. thick. Trim the edges with a sharp knife. Place on a greased baking-sheet and prick the centre with a fork, leaving a margin of ½ in. all round. Fill in the pricked centre thickly with icing sugar. Place stoned fresh plums, cherries or apricots or thinly sliced apples overlapping each other on the pricked space. Sprinkle with more icing sugar and bake for 25-30 minutes in a hot oven (gas mark 7-8 or 450-475 degrees Fahr.).

JODEHGAR (DANISH ALMOND BISCUITS)

> 8 oz. Whitworth's Self-raising Flour
> 4 oz. caster sugar
> 4-5 oz. butter or margarine
> 1 egg
> 1-1½ oz. sugar
> ½ teaspoon ground cinnamon
> 2-3 oz. chopped Whitworth's almonds

Sift the flour and sugar and work in the fat thoroughly. Bind with enough egg to make a dough that's just pliable. Knead well. Roll out to less than ¼ in. thick and cut into rounds. Place on floured baking-sheets and prick all over with a fork. Brush with beaten egg and sprinkle with sugar, cinnamon and chopped almonds. Bake for 15-18 minutes in a moderately hot oven (gas mark 5 or 400 degrees Fahr.).

GERMAN CHEESE CAKE

> Paste:
> 6 oz. Whitworth's Self-raising Flour
> 3 oz. butter or lard
> Pinch of salt
> Milk to mix

116

Filling:

> *1 oz. butter*
> *2-3 oz. caster sugar*
> *2 yolks of egg*
> *1 teaspoon lemon juice*
> *Grated rind of ½ lemon*
> *½ lb. cottage cheese*
> *½ cup evaporated milk*
> *2 whites of egg*

Sift the flour and salt and rub in the fat. Mix to a not-too-stiff paste with milk. Line a pie plate or deepish flan tin with it.

Cream the butter and sugar very well. Then beat in the egg yolks and the lemon juice and rind. Press the cottage cheese through a coarse sieve twice and add with the evaporated milk. Whip the egg whites very stiffly and fold in. Turn into the prepared pastry shell and bake for about 1 hour in a moderate oven (gas mark 4 or 375 degrees Fahr.). Watch and, if necessary, cut down the heat a little.

If you like, sprinkle the top with chopped almonds, a little sugar and ½ teaspoonful ground cinnamon before putting it in the oven. Or mix into the filling a handful or so of Whitworth's sultanas.

You can make your own cottage cheese simply by letting milk sour. Warm it to barely blood heat and drain in a cotton bag. When dry, use the curds as directed.

LINZER TORTE (A GERMAN TART)

> *4 oz. Whitworth's Self-raising Flour*
> *1 oz. cornflour*
> *½ teaspoon ground cinnamon*
> *¼ teaspoon salt*
> *3 oz. butter or margarine*
> *3 oz. Whitworth's ground almonds*
> *3 oz. caster sugar*
> *1 egg*
> *Apricot or other jam*

Sift the first four ingredients and rub the fat into them. Add the ground almonds, sugar and beaten egg. If necessary, a very little milk can be added. Roll out the pastry and line two small or one large shallow sandwich tin with it. Roll off the edges and spread the tart generously with apricot or other jam. Roll out the trimmings, cut in thinnish strips and place them lattice-wise across the jam. Brush the pastry with milk, sprinkle with sugar and bake for 20-25 minutes in a moderately hot oven (gas mark 5 or 400 degrees Fahr.).

PEANUT BUTTER COOKIES (AMERICAN)

½ breakfastcup Whitworth's soft brown sugar
½ breakfastcup caster sugar
½ breakfastcup margarine
1 egg
½ breakfastcup peanut butter
1¼ breakfastcups Whitworth's Self-raising Flour
½ teaspoon bicarbonate of soda
½ teaspoon salt
½ teaspoon vanilla essence

These are rich crumbly "cookies"—very good, and they keep well. Mix the two sugars and cream them with the margarine. Beat in the peanut butter and then the egg and vanilla. Sift flour, soda and salt together and add it to the mixture. Knead well. Roll the dough into small balls. Place them on a greased tin and flatten them with a fork. Bake in a moderately hot oven (gas mark 4-5 or 375-400 degrees Fahr.) for about 15 minutes.

RUSSIAN PIROSHKIS *(Egg and Cabbage)*

Piroshkis are little savoury pastry rolls (like Cornish pasties in miniature), usually eaten with Borsch (beetroot soup) or Stchi (cabbage soup) or as "Zakuski" (hors d'oeuvres). Various pastes are used to make them. We suggest rough puff or short crust pastry (page 8).

½ lb. rough puff or short crust pastry
1½ breakfastcups chopped scalded cabbage
3 hard-boiled eggs
2 walnuts butter
Pinch of salt
Pinch of sugar

Having scalded the cabbage for 5 minutes, press it dry. Chop and add the eggs. Melt the butter, stir in the cabbage and egg with seasoning to taste. Cook for about 10 minutes. Roll out the pastry about ⅛-¼ in. thick and cut into rounds. When filling is cold put portions on each round of pastry, closing them as for Cornish Pasties (page 22). Bake for 15-20 minutes in a fairly hot oven (gas mark 6 or 425 degrees Fahr.).

Another quicker way is to divide the pastry in half, roll each portion out about ⅛ in. thick, keeping the pieces as square as possible. Line a Swiss Roll tin with one piece. Place the prepared filling on it. Damp the edges of the pastry and put the second piece on top, pinching the edges. Brush with beaten egg or milk, prick all over with a fork and bake as above. Cut into suitable pieces.

VIENNA CAKE

> *4 oz. butter or margarine*
> *3 oz caster sugar*
> *2 eggs*
> *6 oz. Whitworth's Self-raising Flour*
> *Pinch of Salt*
> *2-3 tablespoons boiling water*

Grease and flour a 7-in cake tin. Cream the fat and sugar thoroughly— and then cream them again! Beat in the eggs, one at a time, until very light. Work in the sifted flour and salt and, at the last minute, add the boiling water.

Turn into the prepared tin and bake for 40-50 minutes in a moderate oven (gas mark 3-4 or 350-375 degrees Fahr.).

Note.—If the eggs are small, use 3 and slightly reduce the amount of water.

BAKED ALASKA (AMERICAN)

This is quite a spectacular sweet which the children will love. It is very easy to make.

You require a ½-¾ in. thick piece of sponge-cake which can be Victoria Sponge or any of the fatless sponges. It should be the size of the brick of ice cream you are going to use or, if you wish to surround it with fruit, a little larger all round.

It is not necessary to have a refrigerator to keep the ice cream firm. If you have a wide-necked Thermos jar, that is ideal. Take it to the shop where you buy your ice cream and bring it home in it. Several hours later, it will still be hard. Or shop a little later and wrap the ice cream tightly in a piece of old blanket or newspaper which will insulate it very well.

Now that you have the sponge-cake and the ice cream, you are ready for the Baked Alaska.

First, get the oven really hot (gas mark 7-8 or 450-475 degrees Fahr.). Place the layer of cake on a flat oven plate and moisten with fruit juice. For the family-size brick of ice cream, whip 2-3 egg whites very stiffly so that, when you invert the bowl, they will remain in position. Sprinkle over them 1 tablespoon caster sugar (for 2 whites) or 1½ tablespoons (for 3). Whip again to regain the stiffness.

Place the block of ice cream on the sponge with any fruit you want to use on top and around it. Pile the meringue over and around the ice cream and fruit and make sure that it entirely covers them and the cake itself, so that the whole is sealed in, as it were. Have no holes or gaps.

Place towards the top of the oven and bake for 3 minutes, when the meringue will have taken on a lovely golden tint. Remove at once and serve. When the Baked Alaska reaches the table, the ice cream will not be melted in the least—unless, of course, you have not entirely covered it with the meringue.

This sweet is just as good without the fruit.

Sliced fresh or quick-frozen peaches, apricots, pears, or raspberries, strawberries and, indeed, any other fruits are suitable. A very good addition is ginger in syrup.

If fruits in syrup are used, it is very pleasant to moisten the sponge-cake with the syrup, just as you would moisten sponge-cakes in a trifle, Or, if you like, moisten the sponge-cake with a little sherry or cider.

Note.—For ways in which the egg yolks can be used, see Good Cooking Briefs on page 10.

THOUSAND-LEAF TART (SWEDISH)

This is another way of using any of the Flaky Pastries—more attractive, perhaps, than Vanilla Slices because it looks so much better.

After the last rolling-out of any of the flaky pastries, cut into 6-8 equal squares. Roll out each as thinly as possible and then, using a saucepan lid, cut out as large rounds as you can.

Place each on a piece of wax or greaseproof paper on a baking-sheet. (One can bake only two at a time.) Brush with cold water, avoiding the edges. Sprinkle each with a half teaspoon or so caster sugar and bake for 6-8 minutes near the top of a very hot oven (gas mark 7-8 or 450-475 degrees Fahr.). Leave until cold.

The layers are then spread with apple sauce and sweetened whipped cream, in alternate layers and sandwiched, leaving the top layer free. For the top, make a thin white glacé icing (page 84), using a little lemon juice. Finish by making a border of chopped roasted almonds and garnish the centre with a "daisy" of any glace fruit such as candied orange peel, angelica or cherries.

DOBOSCH TORTE (HUNGARIAN)

This very special cake is one of the most famous of the Hungarian "Tortes" and is well worth making now and again. It is made in three parts: the Sponge, the Filling and the Caramel Glaze for the top.

The layers of cake are very thin so, when you make them, just trickle enough batter into the well-greased tins to cover the bottom when the tins are turned this way and that.

> The Sponge:
> *4 oz. caster sugar*
> *4 large eggs*
> *3½ oz. Whitworth's Self-raising Flour*

Beat the sugar and the egg yolks very well together. Gradually stir in the flour and, finally, mix the lightly whipped whites into the mixture. Grease and flour two 6½-7 in. sandwich tins (loose-bottomed ones, for preference). Allow for each only enough batter to cover the bottom. Bake for 5-6 minutes in a moderately hot oven (gas mark 5-6 or 400-425 degrees Fahr.).

As each two layers are baked, simply wipe out the tins, re-grease them and add the batter, as above. Repeat until all is used.

> The Chocolate Butter Filling:
> *4 oz. butter or margarine*
> *4 oz. sugar*
> *1 tablespoon water*
> *1-1½ tablespoons cocoa*

Cut the fat in small pieces into a bowl. Slowly melt the sugar in the water. When it is dissolved, boil without stirring, until a bubble forms when you dip the ring end of a skewer in the syrup and blow through the hole.

Pour the syrup slowly into the fat, stirring all the time, until it becomes a creamy mixture. Stir the cocoa well in, beat well and it is ready.

Reserve the best layer of sponge for the top one, to be added later. Sandwich and top the others with the filling, holding back enough for the sides of the cake.

Note.—For a change, use finely powdered "instant" coffee to taste, instead of cocoa or, if liked, reduce the amount of cocoa and replace it with the coffee powder.

> The Caramel Glaze:

Gradually heat 3 oz. caster sugar in a strong small pan until it becomes a thick syrup. This will become a pale gold and, finally, a rich gold. At this stage, take care not to burn the syrup.

Have the reserved layer of sponge resting on a bread board, and have a palette knife ready in a jug of hot water. When the caramel is a warm gold, pour it all at once on top of the sponge layer and quickly spread it over the entire surface with the palette knife.

Dip a sharp knife in the hot water and quickly mark off the layer into wedges, then cut each through. If the caramel has hardened, it may be necessary to use a weight to hit down on the back of the knife. Lift each wedge and place it neatly on top of the filling, fitting the wedges closely together to re-form the surface.

Leave for a little, then spread the remaining chocolate butter filling on the sides of the cake and cover with chopped walnuts.

ANGEL CAKE (AMERICAN)

2 oz. Whitworth's Self-raising Flour
3½ oz. caster sugar
4-5 egg whites
A good pinch of salt
½ teaspoon vanilla essence
A drop or two almond essence

For this cake, use a "tube" tin—that is, a round tin with a funnel-like tube in the centre. Or use a border mould which is more easy to find. In each case the tin is not greased.

Sift the flour and half the sugar together. Whip the egg whites with the salt until they are fairly stiff but not so dry as for meringues. Sprinkle the remaining sugar over the top, a tablespoonful at a time, and again whip until fairly stiff. Add the essences. Sprinkle the flour and sugar mixture over the surface and fold in lightly with a spoon.

Turn into the tube or border tin and bake for 50-60 minutes in a slowish oven (gas mark 2-3 or 325-350 degrees Fahr.).

Leave in the tin for 5 minutes, then place a wire rack on top and invert the cake on to a table. When it is ready, it will drop on to the rack.

This cake can be iced, though this is not usual. Glacé icing (page 84) or boiled American Frosting (page 80) could be used equally well.

Note.—When Angel Cake is made in a border ring, it is often filled with sweetened fresh fruit and whipped cream or iced cream.

CHILDREN'S HOUR

IN THE KITCHEN

Girls—and boys, too—should learn something about simple cooking while they are small. They'll turn out better wives and more appreciative hubands than will children who are firmly kept out of the kitchen. Let them make toffee by all means—but teach them the secret of a good white sauce and the right way of cooking cabbage, too. Ask for their help when there are eggs to beat, pans to grease, or fruit to clean. If a few sultanas or a lump or two of sugar disappear in the process, it just can't be helped.

RULES FOR BEGINNERS
(1) Start with a clean and tidy kitchen—*and leave it clean and tidy.*
(2) Read your recipe all through before you start and get all the ingredients out. Otherwise there'll be a trail of flour over the floor and sticky marks on the cupboard door.
(3) Measure or weigh very carefully—don't just guess at quantities.
(4) Don't try to hurry your cooking—food can very easily be ruined by too high a temperature.
(5) Even if you're specially fond of anything, don't use too much of it. Too many raisins or too much sugar can spoil a cake instead of making it nicer. Stick to the recipe.

SCRAMBLED EGGS

1 tablespoon butter or margarine
3 eggs (for 2 people)
2 tablespoons top milk or cream
$\frac{1}{8}$ teaspoon salt

Melt the butter or margarine in a small pan or in the top part of a double boiler. Break the eggs into a bowl and beat them only enough to mix them. Add the milk or cream and seasoning. Pour into the melted fat and stir gently until thick. Start dishing up (on hot buttered toast) a few seconds before they are completely thickened—their own heat will finish the job.

BAKED POTATOES

1 large potato apiece
Some bacon rinds or a little melted margarine

Scrub the potatoes well in cold water. Dry them and rub well with bacon rinds or melted margarine. This will make the skins thin and crackly. Bake in fairly hot oven for 45-60 minutes or until you can pierce them with a fork. Make a small cut in each, squeeze to burst the potatoes open, them put a small pat of butter inside each.

Variation: **Potato Surprise**
Cut baked potatoes in half lengthwise and, with a spoon, scoop out most of the inside, leaving about ¼ in. inside the skin all round. Mash the scooped out part with butter or margarine, salt and a little meat or vegetable extract. Return to shells and brown lightly under the grill before serving.

WHITE SAUCE

1 oz. butter or margarine
1 oz. Whitworth's Plain Flour
½-¾ pint milk or other liquid
Pinch of salt
Few grains of pepper

The method is all-important here—you *must* melt the butter or margarine in a small pan, blend in the flour and let the two cook together until they froth. This is called "roux". (Never add flour-and-water to hot liquid—that gives you paste instead of a nice creamy sauce). When cooking your flour and fat, take care not to let it brown. When it's all frothy, remove from the heat and slowly stir in the warm liquid. Very slowly, so as to avoid lumps. Then add the seasonings.
Milk can be used for any white sauce but, if it's a sauce for cauliflower, you can use the liquid in which the cauliflower was cooked; or if it's for chicken, the stock in which the chicken was simmered. At the last moment, you can add a little top milk or cream—but don't let the sauce boil after this has been stirred in.

MARZIPAN *—Needs No Cooking*

> *8 oz. Whitworth's ground almonds*
> *4 oz. caster sugar*
> *4 oz. icing sugar*
> *1 dessertspoon lemon juice*
> *1 teaspoon orange flower water*
> *½ teaspoon vanilla essence*
> *1 white of egg*

With Whitworth's ground almonds, you can make marzipan—and then make lots of lovely sweets with it. Mix the dry ingredients. Add the lemon juice and essences, then add the white of egg, a little at a time, and knead it well into the mixture. If it is too stiff to form into moulds, add a little water, drop by drop, and knead it until you have a good firm paste, soft enough to mould.

COLOURED MARZIPAN

If you like, you can make the marzipan as above, then divide it into three or four lots and colour each with a different colour. For pink marzipan, add the tiniest drop of cochineal to one batch. For green marzipan, add a tiny drop of sap green and, for mauve marzipan, use violet colouring. Simply knead the colourings into the marzipan.

CHOCOLATE "POTATOES"

Form small pieces of marzipan into tiny oval potatoes. Make "eyes" with the end of a skewer, them drop the "potatoes" into cocoa and roll them about in it.
Or make Cinnamon "Potatoes" by rolling them in a mixture of ground cinnamon and icing sugar, half and half.

MARZIPAN FRUITS

Apples: Pinch off small walnuts of marzipan and roll them into rounds in the palms of your hands. Push a clove into one end of each round, to make a calyx. Dilute a few drops of sap green colouring and a few drops of cochineal (in separate saucers) with a little water. Brush these colours on to the "fruit" to give the appearance of small apples.

Strawberries: Shape small pieces of marzipan in the same way and brush them all over with slightly diluted cochineal. Roll them in granulated sugar and place on a wire rack to dry well.

★ *Basic Recipe*

MARZIPAN WALNUTS

Pinch off walnut-sized pieces of marzipan. Roll into small balls. Press half a shelled walnut on each side of each. Place in little paper cases and spoon clear crystallising syrup over each.

To make the crystallising syrup: Put ½ lb. sugar in a strong pan with an eighth of a pint of water. Stir over a low heat until the sugar is dissolved, then boil, without stirring, until a little becomes quite brittle when tested in cold water.

MARZIPAN ALMONDS

Flatten small rounds of marzipan and press half a blanched almond on top of each.

To blanch almonds: Put the almonds in a pan. Cover with cold water and bring to boiling point. Drain and pour cold water over them. The skins will then come off very easily. This is what is called "blanching".

STUFFED DATES

You need dessert dates for these. Make a slit down one side of each and carefully slip out the stone. Pick off hazel nut-size pieces of the marzipan, roll them into date-stone shapes and slip them into the cavities, leaving the marzipan showing. Roll in granulated sugar.

TRUFFLES

Break up a 4-oz. bar of sweet dessert or milk chocolate. Place in a bowl and stand this in hot water until the chocolate is soft. Melt ½ oz. butter and work in as much of it as the chocolate will absorb. Add a few drops vanilla or other flavouring essence. Beat until thick, then form into small balls. Roll in cocoa.

★ CREAMY FUDGE

> 1 teacup top milk
> 1 lb. granulated sugar
> ¼ teaspoon salt
> 2 oz. butter
> ½ teaspoon vanilla essence

First, grease a large shallow tin with butter. Rub over the inside of a *large* aluminium pan with the butter, too. This will help to prevent boiling over.

Pour the milk into the pan, add the sugar and stir over a low heat until the sugar dissolves. *Then do not stir it again.* Boil for 25 minutes rapidly, watching it, because syrup has a way of suddenly "boiling over". Now drop a little from a teaspoon into a cup of cold water. If it forms a firmish ball when tested between the thumb and finger, it is ready for the remaining ingredients. If not, boil a little longer and test again. Then add the salt and butter and stir them in. Adding these now should prevent sticking. When the butter is dissolved, lift the pan on to the kitchen table and leave it there until it is cool enough for you to place your hand comfortably on the bottom of the pan. Add the vanilla essence and at once begin to beat the mixture with a wooden spoon. Continue beating until it thickens and becomes grainy. Turn it into the tin. When it has set, mark it into small squares with the point of a knife.

Here is a tip: If you happen to boil the fudge a moment too long and it becomes "rocky" in the pan while you are beating it, add a teaspoon of hot water, then beat. You may need a little more than a teaspoon of hot water, but try a teaspoon to begin with.

NUT FUDGE

Chop ½ lb. walnuts or almonds and add them to the fudge just before you begin to beat it.

FRUIT NUT FUDGE

Add ¼ lb. each of sultanas and walnuts before beating the fudge.
★ *Basic Recipe*

CHOCOLATE FUDGE

Mix 1 heaped tablespoon cocoa with the dry sugar before combining it with the milk.

★ FONDANT (UNCOOKED) —*Foundation for many sweets*

1 egg white
About 8 oz. icing sugar
Flavouring and colouring to taste

Beat the white of egg. Roll out the icing sugar, sift it through a fine sieve and add it to the beaten white. Work together. Knead to a nice pliable paste, then knead in whatever flavouring and colouring you wish to use. Add more sugar if necessary.

Vanilla Fondants: Work in a little vanilla essence and a drop of cochineal and knead well. Pinch off pieces and roll between the palms. Flatten with half a walnut or half a blanched almond.

Peppermints: Keep the fondant white but flavour it with oil of peppermint.

STUFFED DATES AND OTHER FRUITS

Use this fondant, coloured as desired, for stuffing dates and raisins, in the same way as marzipan is used.

HONEYCOMB TOFFEE

2 oz. Whitworth's Demerara sugar
4 oz. golden syrup
2 level teaspoons bicarbonate of soda

Boil the sugar and syrup together until a rich gold colour. While still boiling, stir the bicarbonate of soda in very quickly. Pour into a well greased sandwich tin and leave to cool and set. When almost firm, loosen edges with a knife and turn out on to a wire tray.

★ *Basic Recipe*

PULLED TOFFEE

> ½ lb. caster sugar
> ⅛ pint water
> 1 tablespoon golden syrup
> ½ teaspoon vinegar
> 1 oz. butter

Put all the ingredients into a large aluminium pan. Bring to the boil and boil without stirring (as this would cause the mixture to "sugar"). When a little becomes quite brittle when dropped into a cup of cold water, pour the toffee into a greased large shallow pan. When it is cool enough to handle, rub butter on your hands and begin to pull it. When you have stretched it as far as you can, fold it and start stretching again. Repeat this until the toffee becomes very difficult to stretch and is a nice blonde colour, then pull to a long strip (or strips) half an inch in diameter. Cut into 1-in. pieces. Wrap in oiled paper and store in tight tins or jars, otherwise it will become sticky.

COCONUT ICE

> 1 lb. granulated sugar
> ½ pint milk
> 6 oz. Whitworth's Desiccated Coconut
> A few drops of red colouring

Into a saucepan put the sugar and milk. Bring to the boil, and boil for 3 minutes. Remove from the heat and add the coconut, and stir until the mixture thickens.
Spread half the mixture into a 7 or 8 in. square buttered tin, colour the remaining half pink and spread on top of the white. Cut into bars when nearly cold.

CURRANTS OR GRAPES, FROSTED

Dip clusters of red or white currants or grapes into a very slightly beaten egg white, then into caster sugar. Remove and leave to dry out.

WEIGHTS and MEASURES

Some women "cook by ear", as it were, and do it beautifully—but, for most of us, it is safer to follow the rule of professional cooks and weigh and measure carefully.

★ To save washing-up, measure dry ingredients first, then use the same spoons or cups for liquids.

★ The British Standards Institution has produced regulation-sized cups, tablespoons and teaspoons which will be invaluable in any kitchen. They were sponsored by the Ministry of Food and your iron-monger can get them for you if they are not already in stock.

★ According to these British Standard measures, 1 cup equals ½ pint; 16 tablespoonfuls equal 1 cupful; 3 teaspoonfuls equal 1 table-spoonful. *Remember that the average teacup holds only about ¼ pint, the average breakfastcup about ½ pint.*

★ To measure syrup easily, lightly grease the spoon or cup first.

★ When the recipe calls for half a teaspoonful or half a tablespoonful, level off your spoon and divide lengthwise with a thin knife.

★ In using scales, see that the food to be weighed see-saws gently with the required weight; neither one side nor the other should stay down.

★ Remember that breadcrumbs and grated cheese weigh less when stale and dry.

All spoonfuls are level ones unless otherwise stated.

What One Half-Pint Cup Weighs

(MINISTRY OF FOOD TABLE)

FOOD	OUNCES
Unsifted Flour	5
Fresh Breadcrumbs . . .	3
Dry Breadcrumbs	6
Cooked Shredded Cabbage .	4
Raw Shredded Cabbage . .	2
Grated Cheese	4
Cocoa	4
Cooking Fat	8
Margarine	8
Oatmeal *(medium)* . . .	8
Rolled Oats	4
Semolina	6
Granulated Sugar	8
Sultanas	6
Syrup	16

How Many Tablespoonfuls to an Ounce?

FOOD	NUMBER OF LEVEL TABLESPOONFULS
Fresh Breadcrumbs . . .	5
Dry Breadcrumbs	3
Grated Cheese	4
Cocoa	3
Cooking Fat	2
Cornflour	3
Unsifted Flour	3
Jam	1
Margarine	2
Oatmeal *(medium)* . . .	2
Rolled Oats	4
Semolina	2½
Syrup	1

Comparative Temperatures

(APPROXIMATE)

Electricity and Gas

ELECTRICITY		GAS
200	Drying temperature	–
225 250	Very slow	– $\frac{1}{4}$
275 300	Slow	$\frac{1}{2}$ 1
325	Moderately slow	2
350 375	Moderate	3 4
400	Moderately hot	5
425 450	Hot	6 7
475 500	Very Hot	8 9

In reading the above temperatures, allowance must be made for any slight variations which may occur, according to make and age of the cooker used.

Index

All spoonfuls are level ones unless otherwise stated

All spoonfuls are level ones unless otherwise stated

All spoonfuls are level ones unless otherwise stated

All spoonfuls are level ones unless otherwise stated